Machine Learning Explained The Simple Way:

A Beginners Guide to Learning Python for
Data Science,
Machine Learning and Ace your Data Science
Interview
With little Coding Experience.

By Santos Ozoemena

SIMPLE CODE
—PUBLISHING—

Table of Contents

INTRODUCTION

"By definition, all scientists are data scientists. In my opinion, they are half hacker, half analyst, they use data to build products and find insights. It's Columbus meets Columbo—starry-eyed explorers and skeptical detectives."

-by Monica Rogati

Are you looking for a career option that guarantees a heavy paycheck? A career that offers massive versatility? A career that ensures an ever-changing and improved job profile? Well then, data science is the only career option that can satisfy all your above desires. If you wish to take control of the future, then data science will help you do that. It is because data scientists are powerful; they are powerful enough to predict any system's future trends precisely. Being a data scientist, you can answer all the questions about the future. Now, what more reason do you want to look into this fascinating topic? The world is changing, thanks to data science. If you wish to cope up and move parallel to the evolving world, you must gear up and enter the enchanting world of data science.

Most of you must have heard about data science and how it is changing the world's dynamics, and you want to discover more about it, however, the problem arises where to start and how to start. Do you stand dumbfounded and maybe alienated to the conversation about data science? Do you want to know more about it, but the complexity of it all makes you reluctant? If your heart beats a chord at any of the above questions, then rest assured. This book will take you down the easiest path to the amazing world of data science. Also, a popular opinion about data science is that people find it too complicated. Well, I would say it is another bogus stereotype. Nothing is too complicated for your brain to understand. Not only this, some people are uncertain why they should learn data science. Some of you might be hesitant to learn about data science because of so many difficult terms related to it. However, your reluctance to learn about data science. Furthermore, if you are looking for a guide to help you learn the basics to continue your coding journey, then this book will be a messiah for you.

This book intends to explain to its readers the true advantage of Data science and Python skills. In a very detailed, yet simple way, this book will become your perfect guide to understand all you need to know about data science. Once you learn more about data science, you can polish your resume and secure a good future career for yourself by learning some highly-in-demand skills. The world we are witnessing right now is a world of the internet, information technology, robotics, and artificial intelligence. You must gear yourself up for the changing current situation where almost every industry is moving towards data science and artificial intelligence. Learning data science will also earn you a competitive edge in the job market. Moreover, this book will help you understand all the ins and outs of Data science and Python coding.

This book is a stepwise guide to help you understand all about data science and machine learning. It aims to resolve all the possible queries and ambiguities that might mist your mind when thinking about data science. The first chapter is all about the basics of data science and the problems it solves. You might have a little prior knowledge of this topic, but as I said before, this book will take your hand from the very beginning till the very end. The chapter will further talk about some solid reasons why you should learn data science and will guide you on how to set up your data science environment.

Moving on, in the second chapter, you will learn in detail about the concepts of machine learning. Machine learning is again a term you might have heard often in your surroundings, so, if you are curious to know more about it, this chapter will pop all your curiosity bubbles. Next is the detailed introduction to Numpy. A powerful library used for scientific computing, Numpy is again the talk of the day. In this chapter, you can learn the basic Numpy arrays and their computation. Moreover, you will explore more into broadcasting arrays, sorting arrays, and indexing in the same chapter.

The following chapter will discuss the concept of Matplotlib and its uses. Also, the chapter contains a wide variety of plots that come with Matplotlib, like line, bar, scatter, histogram, etc. If you are interested in three-dimensional plotting in Matplotlib, then you must have a look at this chapter.

You might have come across the term, 'DataFrame' as they are used immensely in data science, machine learning, and related fields. In its next chapter, this book talks about the Panda DataFrame and how to operate on data in Pandas. The chapter will delve into deeper details like how to handle missing data, the concept of hierarchical indexing, pivot tables, and working with Time Series.

At the next step of the staircase, you will understand SQL, Database concepts, and common interview SQL questions. In this chapter, you will learn about big companies that use SQL, the reason SQL is not going anywhere, the syntax of SQL, and the most frequently asked SQL questions.

This book will talk about Statistics and probability in its next following chapter. You will learn basic stats, the expectations from a data scientist, and common interview questions on statistics. Moreover, you will know how to employ stats in your routine life, and why learning probability is important for data science. In the following chapter, this book aims to uncover the secrets behind predictive modeling. The term may sound complicated, but be at peace, because the previous chapters will equip you with all the pertinent knowledge to understand and comprehend this chapter. You will learn in this chapter, how predictive modeling, machine learning, and statistics are related and different at the same time. In the end, for your better understanding, you will discover some common interview questions in predictive modeling and machine learning.

At last, the final chapter is a case study which will be the final stroke of the brush on the painting. This chapter will provide you with a relevant case study example and its prep.

Now after reading this much, you might be thinking, "Is the author the right person to guide me?". If this question is disturbing you, then the following lines are a must-read. I am a passionate Data Scientist, coder, and programmer. In writing this book, I have authority because I have a strong and unflinching love that goes into becoming an expert coder. While writing a book, it is important to have both passion and knowledge of the subject. I have been studying data science and all its information for years which is why I know what I am talking about. Furthermore, helping you achieve exceptional skills in programming matters to me because what you are about to learn in this book will help you obtain a serious, competitive edge in the market. You can trust me because my experiences and expertise have trained me to become a well-rounded mentor in programming.

The key reason I am writing this book is that I have been once where all beginner programmers and Data scientists were. You cannot expect anyone to snap a finger and become an expert in data science. It all takes effort, and it always begins from block one. I deeply understand the need to learn programming for the job market and want to help beginners reach a level of proficiency.

Now, if your mind is cloudy with intermixing thoughts, then take a deep breath, and grab this book to save you from the overwhelming tides of thoughts. A comprehensive book containing all answers to your confusions, and safe baggage of information regarding data science will give you an edge in the ever-competing and advancing world of science. You might have heard of Darwin's famous theory of survival of the fittest. In the current building scenario, data science and machine learning are quickly taking over the past tools because of their vast applicability. Therefore, if you want to survive and be on the front line, then this book is here to help you out.

A FREE GIFT TO OUR READERS

7 surprising beginner mistakes you should avoid as a
beginner programmer downloadable guideline. This will
set you on the right path to learning how
to program.

santosbooks.com

CHAPTER 1

The BEGINNING OF DATA SCIENCE

What is Data Science?

As we have already established in the introduction that data science is the core of most industries, and all around the globe, currently. Enjoying its position as the hot and most trendy topic of time, data science has made businessmen turn their heads in its direction. So, you may be wondering by now about the true nature of this term, 'data science'. Let us learn all about the basics of data science through this chapter.

In its simplest terms, data science is an interdisciplinary field of study that deals with a colossal amount of structured and unstructured data employing the latest techniques, tools and methods to discover new patterns, thresh out meaningful information, and help making important and intricate business decisions. Moreover, it makes use of complicated machine learning algorithms to create and modify predictive models.

The Data Science Lifecycle

There are five stages of Data science's life cycle:

1. Capture: The main purpose of the first stage is to get the raw material. In this process, data is the raw product. So we will accumulate data first. If you do not have massive data, you cannot proceed to the next steps.

In this stage, you can collect raw structured and unstructured data. You require a Technical skillset like MySQL to obtain the data.

Furthermore, if you are a beginner, you may use Microsoft Excel to collect data and then later convert it into usable data. You can also connect to websites' web servers to obtain data like Facebook and Twitter. Using their web API and then crawling out data are helpful. This stage includes:

- Data acquisition
- Data entry
- Signal reception

2. Maintain: The second stage is also known as the scrubbing stage. In this stage, unnecessary data is filtered that is irrelevant to the analysis. In the maintenance stage, it is necessary to do the following:

- Warehousing
- Cleansing
- Staging
- Processing

- Architecture of data

You have to convert the data from one format to another. Then, you need to merge it all into a standardized format. The second stage is known for transforming the raw information into usable data.

3. Process: In the third stage, the following important things are done:

- Mining
- Summarizing
- Clustering
- Analyzing

Data scientists analyze the patterns and explore the ranges and preferences of the data to determine its effectiveness in predictive analysis.

4. Data Modeling: It is the most important stage of the lifecycle in which all the data modeling is done. Some data scientists believe that it is the real magic.

The prepared data is used to organize the desired output in this process. The following steps are included:

1st Step: Choosing an appropriate machine learning algorithm for the model is required according to the type of data received.

2nd Step: Tuning the hyperparameters of the chosen model is performed to get the best results.

3rd Step: The accuracy and relevance of the model is evaluated.

5. Communication and Model deployment: It is the last stage in which the analyzed data is put into readable charts and graphs. Good and effective communication must be used to deliver the model results to stakeholders.

Most of the stakeholders are not interested in algorithms for the model. They are excited to know how your data model will drive the business world forward.

You might have listened to people around you using the terms machine learning, artificial intelligence with data science. Though subtle, there is a difference among these three terms. It is important first to learn to distinguish the three terms and learn their peculiarities.

1. Artificial Intelligence: This term refers to getting a computer to imitate the behavior of humans.

2. Data Science: This is an umbrella category of artificial intelligence; it incorporates scientific methods and data analysis to get meaning and useful insight from data.

3. Machine learning: This term is another subcategory of artificial intelligence; it uses techniques that allow computers to observe and analyze the data and then carry out artificial intelligence applications. This term will be further discussed in the next chapter.

Data Science is the core foundation to learning

❏ Machine Learning

❏ Artificial Intelligence (A.I)

❏ Advanced-Data Analytics

❏ Advanced Statistics

We have already learned about the first two terms; now let us discover the other two.

1. Advanced-Data Analytics:

In the simplest terms, advanced data analytics is a term which includes all the high-level tools and methods to help you squeeze out the most information out of data. Advanced data analytics also has predictive power which can help you forecast events and trends. The predictive capability can be of great help to organizations as they can analyze future trends in the business and eradicate all possible risks.

Data mining is a vital aspect of advanced data analytics. In this automated process, usable information is extracted from large amounts of raw data. Advanced data analytics is a vast combination of analytical methods which aids businesses in finding and analyzing data trends by making use of data-driven statistics. These techniques include machine learning, data mining, forecasting, visualization, cluster analysis.

Businesses extract the most out of these advanced data analytics techniques because it strengthens their perspective and planning approach. Moreover, it improves their forecast and helps them in making better decisions. Such techniques help develop agility in business actions. Last but not the least, such methods reduce the risk of frauds and other collateral damages.

SOME FAMOUS EXAMPLES OF DATA SCIENCE

1. STREAMING SERVICES: All of us, in the current times, make use of online services. You stream online videos, movies and songs, but have you ever wondered the engine behind these huge streaming services like Netflix, Hulu, or Spotify?

You might not know but data science plays the key role in bringing more happy customers to these online platforms by making their experience worthwhile. Data science gives the streaming businesses a vivid analysis of consumers' taste and experience in the form of charts and graphs. After having better information about the consumers' choice, the services are molded in a way that brings in more customer attraction.

Through use of data science, machine learning, and deep learning, online movie platforms like Netflix have grown exponentially. Netflix, despite its competition in the market, is able to secure most viewers through subscription method and account sharing technique. Established for years, this huge streaming business has gathered heaps of data about its consumers. You might be surprised to hear that the data is about the age, gender, place of living, and the tastes of the customers; the list goes even longer. Through gathering this individualistic data, Netflix provides services to each customer according to his own taste. Now you might be able to answer how Netflix gives you recommendations that just suit *your* preferences. So, before you even finish watching a movie, Netflix dives into your brain, and then offers the best movie you might like to see next.

We have data that suggests there is different viewing behavior depending on the day of the week, the time of day, the device, and sometimes even the location.

- Reed Hastings (CEO Netflix)

You must be wondering how Netflix and other streaming businesses collect, analyze and then utilize this vast data to help generate useful insights about the consumers and give out better results. Streaming services use various algorithms and mechanisms to make use of the heaps of data it has collected.

Near Real-Time Recommendations Engine is one such tool. The ratings that each individual gives on Netflix is added to the collection of Big Data stored in their database. Using these ratings and comments and using key learning algorithms, a fixed pattern is generated which is separate for each individual. It is because everyone's taste is unique, the pattern formed is also unique. So, the recommendation system suggests a preferable list of videos, songs or movies to watch.

"Netflix will know everything. Netflix will know when a person stops watching it. They have all of their algorithms and will know that this person watched five minutes of a show and then stopped. They can tell by the behavior and the time of day that they are going to come back to it, based on their history."

- Mitchell Hurwitz

Metaflow, Polynote, Metacat, Druid, and use of Python have made these online streaming services much more compatible and customer-friendly.

2. ECOMMERCE BUSINESS AND DATA SCIENCE

There are some amazing ways in which data science is changing, improving the world of ecommerce. Popular online shopping sites like Amazon and eBay keep a record of all the clicks you make on their sites and gather data of your shopping taste and experience. Using data science, these sites give personalized product recommendations.

Amazon is an example of this, 'Amazon Personalize' to generate individual product recommendations to ease customers and to increase sales. It has been calculated that 35% of revenue comes from Amazon's recommendation engine. According to a Barilliance report, 31% of revenue is generated through recommendation engines in the worldwide eCommerce industry.

3. HEALTHCARE AND DATA SCIENCE

Data science has made medical Image Analysis a crucial part of healthcare. Whether doctors need to check for tumors, or perform organ delineation, data science technology comes to the rescue. Methods like Deep Learning are used to find best ways to carry out tasks like lung texture classification.

Data science has helped scientists to improve their research in genetics and genomics. Scientists are using data science techniques to find the impact of DNA on human health and the relationship between drug response, diseases and genetics. Moreover, it helps combine different data with genomic data to help in the disease research, this can in turn help the scientists to analyze the genetic issues in reaction to different drugs and diseases.

The financial costs, lab tests, and the waiting time are factors which make drug development take years. However, data science and machine learning has made this process quicker. Screening of drug products in the start or the prediction of success rate are processes which take too much time. However, data science, through advanced mathematical modeling and other forecasting algorithms has made the process much more efficient and accurate.

WHY SHOULD YOU LEARN DATA SCIENCE?

1. Data Science is the career of tomorrow

With technology increasing by leaps and bounds, more and more industries, all over the world, are becoming data-driven. Data science has successfully made its place unchallenged in the coming future. The engine behind this evolving technology is the use of data science in almost all economies, institutions and businesses. By understanding global patterns, consumers' choice and emerging trends, data science has made the future of businesses more secure than ever. Many companies who have not yet switched to data science methods completely, have instead made small data science units to work on analytics. You might be surprised to hear that it is predicted that data science platforms will reach approximately 178 billion USD by the year 2025. So, the world of tomorrow is surely the world of data science.

There is a high demand for data scientists with an ever-increasing scope of data science. The reason is obvious. When big industries continue to generate more data, there is a high demand for data scientists to analyze both structured and unstructured data. Data scientists are also required in assisting the business companies in making smarter decisions and creating better and satisfactory products for the customers.

In the world of data science, it has become increasingly important to possess data literacy. We must learn the process of transforming the raw data into usable and meaningful products. Also, we should learn the methods and requirements to analyze and then draw useful insight from that data. Most of the job roles, in current times, require data handling as the main skill.

2. Data science is one of the most lucrative careers you can opt for

A Glassdoor study revealed that the average salary for a data scientist is $117,345 which is above the national average of $44,564. In even simpler terms, as a data scientist you can make 163% more than the national average salary. Now, you may know why being a data scientist can earn you success, fame and lots of money. The reality is that currently there is a scarcity of data Scientists and this is the reason there is a huge income bubble.

The learning curve of data science is quite steep because this interdisciplinary field requires a person to have knowledge and proficiency in various fields like Statistics, Mathematics, and Computer Science. Therefore, the market value of a data scientist is very high. Adding to the value, the pay scale of a data scientist is way above other IT and management sectors. However, one thing to keep in mind is that the salary of data scientists is just the proportional amount of work that they should put in. Data science is not just a simple field; it requires skills and hard work.

As a data scientist, you can always expect the most prestigious position in the company. Data scientists are relied upon by the company to make them steer into the right direction and help them make data-driven decisions. Not only this, the role of the Data scientist depends on the specialization of his employer company. For example – A commercial industry will require a data scientist to analyze their sales.

3. Basic Data science skills are important for personal use.

It is not that data science only helps those looking for jobs. In our daily routines, owning some basic data science skills can make our lives easier. You must be aware of online shopping. Are you? The famous Amazon earned billions during the pandemic as the online shopping trend skyrocketed. While shopping online, it is important to analyze the maximum, minimum and average price of an item from all online retailers, which can be done only if you know how to analyze sales data. Using this kind of data analysis, you can understand if you are paying too much for an item or not.

Teachers can better analyze the test scores of their students by using data science techniques. I use my data science knowledge to build models for personal use such as a home buying recommender system (to predict housing price based on predictors such as a number of rooms, square footage, age of the house, zip code, etc.), mortgage

calculator, etc.

4. Generate side income using Data science.

Generating side income through data science is no dream now. There are many ways you can earn additional money if you have a data science background by opting for freelancing, tutoring, teaching or blogging. In the beginning, I earned little money, $2 per month on my data science articles. Now, I earn $600 a month from my articles, certainly not house rent yet, but quite a good subsidiary income, especially as it is generated from something I love doing. No success can be gained from shortcuts; Data science is a field that can earn you lots of money, but it never guarantees overnight success. So, learn some basics of data science and start earning money.

Regardless, the ideas I'm about to suggest would certainly help you upskill, earn a good side income as a data scientist, and most importantly, be your own boss.

● Writing articles

● Participating in Kaggle competitions

● Doing freelance work

● Teaching

● Starting a YouTube Channel

5. Data Science will help you earn problem-solving skills.

Problem solving is a skill not easy to learn; it is a step wise process which will first help you learn to deal with smaller problems and then the bigger ones. Solving problems will distill greater confidence in you, and make you progress in life. Data science, python and machine learning teaches you the flair of problem solving. The power to think analytically and approach problems in the right way is a skill that's always useful, not just in the professional world, but in everyday life as well.

Problem solving technique also helps you believe in your ability to think mathematically and analytically. Problem-solving develops mathematical power. It gives students the tools to apply their mathematical knowledge to solve hypothetical and real-world problems.

6. Python and Data Science are in crazy demand.

If you are applying for a data-related job, then having Python with data science on your CV can give you a huge boost. In today's age, it is very rare that individuals have both python and data science skills; it is either Python or Data Science. So, if you have skills in both the fields, then it can give you an edge in the job market, and will make you stand out from other competitors.

HOW TO SET UP YOUR DATA SCIENCE ENVIRONMENT?

Before we move on to the step wise process of the data science environment, we need to learn what a data science environment is. It is the collection of relevant software and hardware in which the program executes. For example, if you are running a videogame with an intensive and intricate software on your outdated computer, then it is highly probable that your computer will slow down, or in worst cases, crash. It is because the environment which suited the video game was not provided by your computer.

1. Python and The Anaconda Package Management System.

Python is the top language used for data science and one of the fastest growing among all programming languages. It is believed that python's popularity owes to the ease with which it can be learned. In this section, we will use the Python programming language to solve data science problems. Also, we will look at the software and hardware requirements and the complete installation and setup details.

Software Requirements: For the best student experience, we recommend the following hardware configs.

● OS: Windows 7 SP1 64-bit, WIndows 8.1

64-bit or Windows 10 64-bit, Ubuntu Linux,

or the latest version of OS X

● Browser: Google Chrome/Mozilla Firefox
Latest Version

● Notepad++/Sublime Text as IDE (this is
optional, as you can practice everything
using jupyter Notebook on your browser)

● Python 3.4+ (latest is PYTHON 3.7)
installed from https://python.org)

● Python Libraries as needed (Jupyter,
Numpy, Pandas, Matplotlib and so on)

❑ Hardware Requirements: For the best student
experience, we recommend the following hardware
configs

● Processor: Intel Core i5 or equivalent

● Memory: 4 GB RAM

● Storage: 35 GB available space

Installation and Setup: Before you start this book make sure you have installed the anaconda environment as we will be using the Anaconda

distribution of python.

● Installing Anaconda: Install Anaconda by the following instruction:

- You must install offline copies of both docs.anaconda.com and enterprise-docs.anaconda.com by installing the conda package anaconda-docs:

  conda install anaconda-docs

- You must install offline copies of documentation for many of Anaconda's open-source packages by installing the conda package anaconda-oss-docs:

  conda install anaconda-oss-docs

- Qt and other packages released after Anaconda Distribution 5.1 (February 15th, 2018) may not work on macOS 10.9, so it may be necessary to not update certain packages beyond this point.
- Install Anaconda to a directory path that does not contain spaces or unicode characters.
- Do not install as Administrator unless admin privileges are required.

- If you did not download to your Downloads directory, replace `~/Downloads/` with the path to the file you downloaded.
- We recommend you accept the default install location. Do not choose the path as /usr for the Anaconda/Miniconda installation.

CHAPTER 2

INTRODUCTION TO MACHINE LEARNING

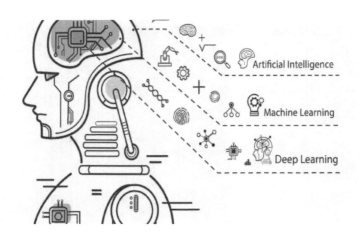

WHAT IS MACHINE LEARNING?

As we have established it before, most people confuse machine learning with data science, or even often, some call it a subcategory of data science, but for beginners, this introduction to machine learning can prove to be a little misleading. To put it in a few simple words, machine learning deals with building models of data.

Mathematical models are built in order to better and deeply understand data and decode it in all possible and useful ways. Models are located with different tunable parameters and then the program is made to 'learn' from the data. Models are first fitted to a seen data. After that it is used to analyze and predict the trends in the new data.

There are two major categories of machine learning to which you should be familiar at this stage.

1. Supervised Learning: In this category, relationships between measured features of data and some labels related to the data are modeled. Once model determining is done, the information can attach labels to new and unfamiliar data. This category is further divided into *classification* and *regression* tasks. In classification, labels are separate categories whereas in regression, labels are continuous quantities.

2. Unsupervised Learning: In this category, features of a data set are modeled without a reference to any label. This type of learning is often described as 'letting the dataset speak for itself.' Clustering and Dimensionality reduction are two subdivisions of unsupervised learning. In clustering, algorithms classify distinct clusters of data whereas in reduction, algorithms look for more brief representations of data.

There is also semi-supervised learning which, as the name suggests, falls somewhere between supervised and unsupervised learning. It comes handy when there are unidentified labels.

MACHINE LEARNING VS DATA SCIENCE

Before we move on to the details of machine learning, it is important to learn the key differences between the two terms: data science and machine learning.

Data science: It is an interdisciplinary field of study which takes a scientific approach to extract useful insight from the data. Data scientists need to be equipped with a unique combination of skills and experience. For example, one must be fluent in programming languages like Python and R; one must have knowledge of statistical methods, a deep understanding of database architecture, and most of all, knowledge and practice to apply this understanding and skills to real-world problems. As it is quite useless to have all the experience of data science without having any knowledge of how to incorporate it in a real-world situation.

With all its glory and supremacy, data science has certain limitations as well. As the functioning of data science purely depends on data, if the data is messy, small and incorrect, it can waste a lot of time. It will create models that generate meaningless and ambiguous results. Moreover, if the data does not sense the real reason behind variation, data science is useless.

Machine learning: It refers to various methods and tools employed by data scientists that permit computers to 'learn' from data. These methods generate results which perform exceptionally well without the need for programming rules.

Machine learning creates a useful model through testing various solutions against the given data and then searching the best solution for the problem. Therefore, problems which are highly labor intensive for us are taken good care of by machine learning. In a very efficient and reliable manner, machine learning can make predictions, and upon those predictions, make the best decision even of most complex issues.

This is the reason that most of the industries are now switching to machine learning as their main drive. Due to its vast possibilities, machine learning has the potential to even rescue endangered lives by solving critical problems in healthcare organizations. Machine learning algorithms have successfully cut many organizations' big costs by making useful decisions to solve problems.

However, there are certain limitations to machine learning as well. Even though its algorithms are quite useful in producing useful insights, we may still require programmers who can enhance the algorithms to make them solve newer problems. Also, in some cases, if we add machine learning to a problem that could be solved by traditional methods, it can complicate it further instead of solving it the simpler way.

One thing to keep in mind is that data science is a very vast term including many branches, and machine learning is one of its branches. Though not allowed to be mixed or interchanged, these two terms are related to a degree where data science is the umbrella term for machine learning. However, both have separate qualities and functions and both require a distinct skillset. Now let us look at the skills required in both machine learning and data science.

a. Skills required in Data science:

I.	Statistics
II.	Data mining and cleaning
III.	Data visualization
IV.	Unstructured data management techniques
V.	Programming languages such as R and Python
VI.	Understand SQL databases
VII.	Use big data tools like Hadoop, Hive and Pig

b. Skills required in Machine Learning

I. Understanding of Computer science fundamentals

II. Statistical modeling

III. Knowledge of Data evaluation and modeling

IV. Understanding and application of algorithms

V. Natural language processing and its application

VI. Data architecture design

VII. Text representation techniques

AN INTRODUCTION TO SCIKIT-LEARNING

Scikit-Learn is one of the best Python libraries which can give a concrete application of a range of machine learning algorithms. Scikit-Learn is a package that can offer effective versions of a wide range of some commonly-used algorithms. The most famous and widely-known characteristics of Scikit-Learn is its unvarying and streamlined API and full online documentation. The API is highly beneficial once you understand the basic concept of Scikit-Learn for any single model, you can easily switch to a new model or algorithm.

DATA REPRESENTATION IN SCIKIT-LEARN

First, let us look into how data can be represented so it can be understood by the computer. The best way to understand data representation is in tabular form.

1. Data in a tabular form:

The most commonly-used table is a two-dimensional grid of data. In this table, individual elements of the data set are written in the rows whereas the columns represent quantities which are related to the elements given in the rows. Generally, rows and columns of the matrix are called samples. Number of rows are *n-samples* and the number of columns are *n-features*. Below is given a famous Irish dataset which was analyzed by Ronald Fisher in 1936.

In [1]
import **seaborn as sns**
iris = sns.load_dataset('iris')
iris.head()

Out[1]:

	sepal_length	sepal_width	petal_length	petal_width	species
0	5.1	3.5	1.4	0.2	setosa
1	4.9	3.0	1.4	0.2	setosa
2	4.7	3.2	1.3	0.2	setosa
3	4.6	3.1	1.5	0.2	setosa
4	5.0	3.6	1.4	0.2	setosa

2. Features Matrix

The table layout which you saw above shows that information can be taken as a two-dimensional numerical array or matrix, which can be simply referred to as a features *matrix*. Conventionally, the feature matrix is stored in an X named variable. This two-dimensional matrix is mostly contained in a NumPy array or a Pandas DataFrame

The samples (i.e., rows) represent the individual objects described by the dataset. The features (i.e., columns) refer to the distinct observations that label every sample quantitatively.

3. Target array

Other than the feature matrix 'x', we work with a target array called 'y'. Unlike the features matrix, it is one-dimensional with lengths referred to as 'n_samples' and is contained in a NumPy array or Pandas series. 'Y' may contain continuous numerical values or separate, distinct labels.

One distinct feature that separates target arrays from other feature columns is that it is most often the quantity which we desire to make predictions about from the data: to state it in statistical terms, it is the dependent variable.

The expected layout of both features and target arrays is presented in the below given diagram.

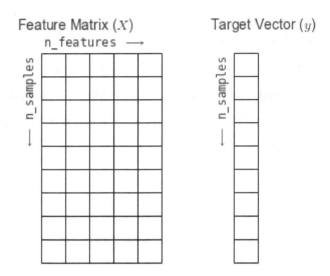

ESTIMATOR API OF SCIKIT-LEARN

There are certain guiding principles which should be kept in mind while studying the design of the Scikit-Learn API.

a. **Consistency**: All objects having consistent documentation share a mutual interface that is deduced from a limited set of methods.

b. **Inspection**: All discrete parameter values are visible as public attributes.

c. **Limited object hierarchy**: Python classes represent algorithms only. Datasets are displayed in standard formats (NumPy arrays, Pandas DataFrames, SciPy sparse matrices). Moreover, parameter names use standard Python strings.

d. **Composition:** Most of the machine learning tasks can be displayed as sequences of more essential algorithms.

e. **Sensible defaults**: The library allocates suitable default values when the models require user-specified parameters.

API'S BASICS

The steps in using Scikit-Learn estimator API are given below:

1. First, choose a model class by importing the suitable estimator class from Scikit-Learn.

2. Then choose hyperparameters of models.

3. Assemble data into target vector and features matrix.

4. Fit the model according to your data.

5. Apply that model to new data.

For supervised learning, we use predict () method to predict labels for unknown data.

For unsupervised learning, we can use either transform () or predict () method to transform or infer properties of the data. often transform or infer properties of the data using the transform () or predict () method.

HYPERPARAMETERS AND MODEL VALIDATION

In order to use these tools and techniques effectively, two steps are extremely important. These two steps are choosing a class of model and model hyperparameter. Also, we need some method to ensure that our chosen model and hyperparameter are valid.

Model validation is not a very intricate task. All you need to do is choose a model and its hyperparameter and then estimate how efficient and valid it is by applying it on training data and then comparing the prediction to the known value. Let us discuss some effective approaches to model validation.

1. HOLDOUT SETS

In a holdout set, we keep or hold back a subset of the data from the training of the model and afterwards utilize that holdout set to evaluate the performance of the model. In Scikit Learn, there is a tool known as *train_test_split* which can be used to split the holdout subset from the rest of the data.

In [5]:
from sklearn.cross_validation import train_test_split
 # split the data with 50% in each set
X1, X2, y1, y2 = train_test_split(X, y, random_state=0,
                        train_size=0.5)

```
# fit the model on one set of data
model.fit(X1, y1)

# evaluate the model on the second set of data
y2_model = model.predict(X2)
accuracy_score(y2, y2_model)
```

Out[5]:
0.90666666666666662

In this example, we can see a more logical result obtained. The nearest-neighbor classifier is highly accurate (about 90%) on this hold-out set. Here too, the hold-out set is the same as unknown data for the reason that it is 'unseen' to the model.

2. CROSS-VALIDATION

There is a drawback of using a holdout set: a portion of data is lost to the model training. In the example we have seen above, almost half of the dataset has no contribution in the training of the model.

Therefore, cross-validation comes for the rescue. In this approach, you perform a sequence of fits where every subset of the data is used, simultaneously, as a training set and as a validation set.

FEATURE ENGINEERING

Feature learning is one of the crucial steps one must learn during machine learning practice. In this process, you learn to build your feature matrix by taking all information you have about your problem and then turning it into numbers. Now let us see some common examples of feature engineering.

1. CATEGORICAL FEATURES

There are other easier ways to interpret data in a simple and predictable way other than presenting data in the form of numbers. Numerical data is not of much help in scikit-learn methods. However, data encryption through the process of *one-hot encoding* is an efficient method of representing quantitative data. This method uses only two digits for encoding its data, which are 0 and 1.

Example of this simplification is found in our computers which uses bits and bytes to convert such heavy numerical data into only a two-digit system.

Such a feature is usually split into a set of features. For example, gender according to the ISO/IEC 5218 standard can take one of four values: not known, male, female, and not applicable.

TEXTUAL FEATURES

This incorporates converting textual values into numerical data which can be helpful in encoding some confidential information by converting it into numbers. *Word count* is an example of such a feature, which helps presenting your data in a precise form.

3. IMAGE FEATURES

Image features come in handy when you want to befittingly encode images for machine learning analysis. Using the pixel value is the simplest approach.

4. DERIVED FEATURES

Derived features, as the name suggests, are mathematically derived from various input features. One example is constructing polynomial features from your input data. Through derived features, we can bring improvement to the model by not changing the whole model, but just transforming the inputs.

NAÏVE BAYES CLASSIFICATION

These models are a group of highly fast and simple classification algorithms that can deal with high-dimensional datasets. They can come in handy as a quick-and-dirty baseline for a classification problem as these models are fast and have very less tunable parameters. Let us see how naïve Bayes classifiers work and a few examples.

If you wish to understand naïve Bayes classifiers, you must understand Bayesian classification methods. First, you should know about Bayes's theorem: it is an equation which describes the relationship of conditional probabilities of statistical quantities. In this classification, we find the probability of a label which has certain observed features; we can write it as P(L | features). Bayes's theorem helps us in expressing this in terms of quantities and which can be computed more directly.

$$P(L \mid \text{features}) = \frac{P(\text{features} \mid L)}{P(L)P(\text{features})}$$

1. GAUSSIAN NAÏVE BAYES

In the easiest to understand naïve Bayes classifier, the assumption we make is: *data from each label is drawn from a simple Gaussian distribution.* One of the fastest and simplest ways to make a model asks for an assumption that data is described by Gaussian distribution having no covariance between dimensions.

2. MULTINOMIAL NAÏVE BAYES

In multinomial naïve Bayes, features are assumed to be produced from a simple multinomial distribution. This type of distribution explains the probability of observing counts among various categories. Therefore, features which represent counts or count rates mostly make use of multinomial naïve Bayes.

LINEAR REGRESSION

Simpler linear regression assists us in plotting scattered data into straight line fit to data. Straight line data is represented by the formula:

$$y = ax + b$$

a refers to the slope, which shows an inclined behavior. Whereas **b** refers to the intercept, which depicts those points in the graph crossing the axes. This model is usually known as *slope-intercept form.*

Scikit learning can be helpful in linear regression in plotting a straight line fit to data.

Trailing underscore method is used to avoid conflicts with the keywords, so in scikit learn slope and intercept are replaced by trailing underscore. So here applicable variables are **coef** and **intercept**.

Linear regression helps minimize discrepancies in input and output values. It is not only useful in simple straight line fit but also in compound variables which are an intricate set of variables.

$$y = a_0 + a_1x_1 + a_2x_2 + \ldots$$

Multidimensional variables can be difficult to understand but NumPy's matrix multiplication operator is useful in this situation.

Three arbitrary values of **x** establish data of **y**.

However, linear regressions are apparently restricted to linear variable relationships.

SUPPORT VECTOR MACHINES

Support vector machines (SVMs) are a strong and conveniently flexible class of supervised algorithms and are used in both classification and regression problems. In this section, we will discuss discriminative classification. In this type of classification, instead of modeling every single class, we find a curve or line in two dimensions or a manifold in multiple dimensions that makes the division in classes.

In the example below there is a simplified case of a classification problem; the two classes of points are separated from one another.

In [1]:
```
%matplotlib inline
import numpy as np
import matplotlib.pyplot as plt
from scipy import stats

# use seaborn plotting defaults
import seaborn as sns; sns.set()
```

In [2]:
```
from sklearn.datasets.samples_generator import
make_blobs
X, y = make_blobs(n_samples=50, centers=2,
                  random_state=0, cluster_std=0.60)
plt.scatter(X[:, 0], X[:, 1], c=y, s=50,
cmap='autumn');
```

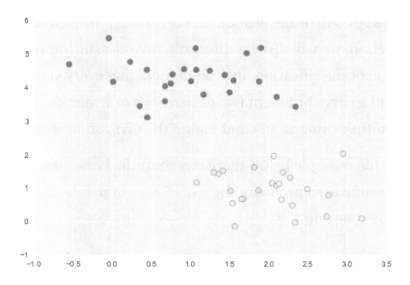

In the case of a linear discriminative classifier, you would see a straight line which splits the two sets of data, and thus, building a model for classification. However, in the above example, there is an issue. If you observe closely, you will see that there can be more than one dividing line that can flawlessly differentiate between the two classes.

We can draw them as follows:

In [3]:
xfit = np.linspace(-1, 3.5)
plt.scatter(X[:, 0], X[:, 1], c=y, s=50, cmap='autumn')
plt.plot([0.6], [2.1], 'x', color='red', markeredgewidth=2,
markersize=10)

```
for m, b in [(1, 0.65), (0.5, 1.6), (-0.2, 2.9)]:
    plt.plot(xfit, m * xfit + b, '-k')
```

plt.xlim(-1, 3.5);

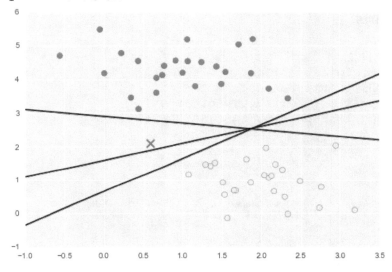

Above, you can see three completely different separators which can perfectly distinguish between the samples. A new data point (which is marked X in the plot) will be given a new label according to your choice of separator.

Evidently our simple intuition of "drawing a line between classes" is not enough, and we need to think a bit deeper.

DECISION TREES AND RANDOM FORESTS

Another powerful and non-parametric algorithm is called *random forests*. An example of ensemble method, it depends upon accumulation of results of an ensemble of simple estimators. Often, using such ensemble methods, we can get astonishing results as the sum value can be larger than the parts.

In [1]:
```
%matplotlib inline
import numpy as np
import matplotlib.pyplot as plt
import seaborn as sns; sns.set()
```

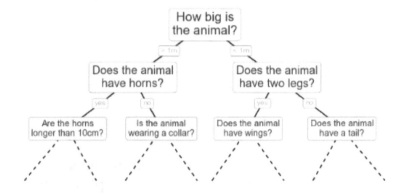

In [2]:
```
from sklearn.datasets import make_blobs

X, y = make_blobs(n_samples=300, centers=4,
                  random_state=0, cluster_std=1.0)
plt.scatter(X[:, 0], X[:, 1], c=y, s=50,
cmap='rainbow');
```

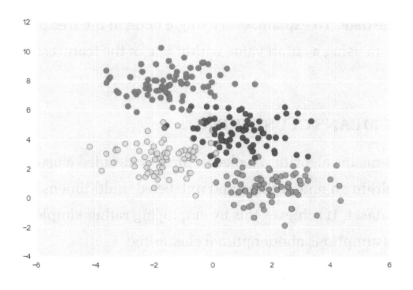

Decision trees are highly spontaneous ways to label or categorize objects. All you need to do is ask a series of questions which are constructed to zero-in on the classification. Binary splitting in the decision trees increases their efficiency. In a well-formed decision tree, every question will reduce the number of options roughly by half. Therefore, even if you have a large number of classes, you can narrow down your options quickly.

Decision trees, when applied in machine learning, have questions that usually take the form of axis-aligned splits in the data. To explain, every single node in the tree halves the data using a cutoff value within one of the features.

K-MEANS CLUSTERING

K-means algorithm looks for already-decided cluster numbers within an unidentified and unlabeled multidimensional dataset. It achieves this by employing rather simple assumptions about optimal clustering:

1. The "cluster center" refers to the arithmetic mean of all the points which belong to the cluster.

2. Each point is nearer to its own cluster center than to other cluster centers.

The above given assumptions make the foundation of the k-means model.

EXPECTATION-MAXIMIZATION IN K-MEANS ALGORITHM

Expectation-maximization is a highly stable and firm algorithm which is explained in data science in various contexts. K-means is a relatively easier and simple-to-understand usage of the algorithm. To explain succinctly, E-M approach consists of this process:

1. Guess a few cluster centers

2. Keep repeating until it converges

   1. E-Step: allocate the points to its nearest cluster center

   2. M-Step: establish the cluster centers to the mean.

In [1]:
```
%matplotlib inline
import matplotlib.pyplot as plt
import seaborn as sns; sns.set()   # for plot styling
import numpy as np
```

In [2]:
```
from sklearn.datasets.samples_generator import
make_blobs
X, y_true = make_blobs(n_samples=300, centers=4,
                       cluster_std=0.60,
random_state=0)
plt.scatter(X[:, 0], X[:, 1], s=50);
```

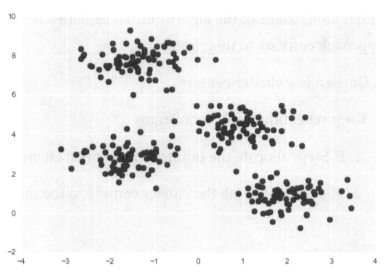

In [3]:
```
from sklearn.cluster import KMeans
kmeans = KMeans(n_clusters=4)
kmeans.fit(X)
y_kmeans = kmeans.predict(X)
```
Let's visualize the results by plotting the data colored by these labels. We will also plot the cluster centers as determined by the *k*-means estimator:

In [4]:
```
plt.scatter(X[:, 0], X[:, 1], c=y_kmeans, s=50,
cmap='viridis')

centers = kmeans.cluster_centers_
plt.scatter(centers[:, 0], centers[:, 1], c='black',
s=200, alpha=0.5);
```

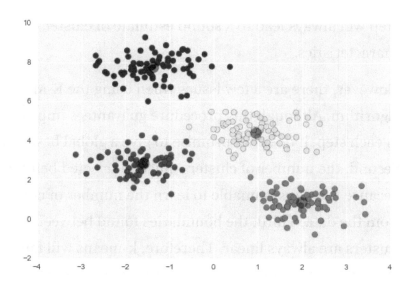

Above, the E-Step is the "Expectation" step because it is responsible for updating our expectation of where each cluster belongs. On the other hand, M-Step is the "Maximization" step because it maximizes the fitness function that tells the location of each location cluster. In this example, that maximization is achieved by simply taking the mean of the data found in each cluster.

There are vast characteristics of this literature, but to summarize some important ones, we can conclude that in normal situations, repetition of both the E-Step and the M-

Step will always lead to a sound estimate of cluster characteristics.

However, there are a few issues when using the E-M algorithm. Although this procedure guarantees improvement in each step, it does not promise to give a global best solution. Second, the number of clusters must be selected beforehand because *k-means* is unable to learn the number of clusters from the data. Third, the boundaries found between K-means clusters are always linear. Therefore, k-means will fail to operate for more intricate boundaries. Last, as the number of samples increases, efficiency of k-means can grow slower because each repetition of k-means must have access to every point in the dataset.

A FACE DETECTION PIPELINE: A REAL-WORLD APPLICATION

Real-world datasets are not that simple and homogenous as we have learnt so far; they are noisy, have missing features, and top of all, they may contain data which is very hard to map to a clean matrix. Therefore, before applying any method, a data scientist must first use his intuition and professional insight to extract these features from the data.

Among many other applications of machine learning, image application is the most compelling to me. In the past, we have seen a few instances in which pixel-level features were used for classification. In the practical world, data is mostly non-uniform, and so, simple pixels are not suitable.

Let us look at one of the feature extraction techniques: Histogram of Oriented Gradients (HOG). This technique changes image pixels into a vector representation without taking in account perplexing factors like illumination. Using these features and certain machine learning algorithms, we will compose a simple face detection pipeline.

HOG FEATURES

Some main steps which are involved in HOG procedure are summarized below:

1. To resist dependence on variations in illumination, you may pre-normalize images.

2. Using two filters that are sensitive to horizontal and vertical brightness gradients, convolve the two images. You can get contour, edge, and texture information in this step.

3. Now split the image into cells of prearranged size, and then program a histogram of the gradient orientations in every cell.

4. Compare the histograms to the block of neighboring cells; therefore, normalizing them. By completing this step, you can further cut down the effect of illumination.

5. Taking information from every cell, form a one-dimensional feature vector.

USING HOG AS A SIMPLE FACE DETECTOR

We can create a simple facial detection algorithm, using the HOG features with Scikit-Learn estimator. When using the linear support vector machine, the steps are given below:

1. First, to obtain "positive" training samples, get a set of image thumbnails of faces.

```
from sklearn.datasets import fetch_lfw_people
faces = fetch_lfw_people()
positive_patches = faces.images
positive_patches.shape
Out[1] (13233, 62, 47)
```

2. Second, to obtain "negative" training samples, get a set of image thumbnails of non-faces. We can use some of the images shipped with Scikit-Image, along with Scikit-Learn's PatchExtractor:

In [4]:

```python
from skimage import data, transform

imgs_to_use = ['camera', 'text', 'coins', 'moon',
    'page', 'clock', 'immunohistochemistry',
    'chelsea', 'coffee', 'hubble_deep_field']
images = [color.rgb2gray(getattr(data, name)())
    for name in imgs_to_use]
```

In [5]:

```python
from sklearn.feature_extraction.image import PatchExtractor

def extract_patches(img, N, scale=1.0,
patch_size=positive_patches[0].shape):
    extracted_patch_size = tuple((scale *
np.array(patch_size)).astype(int))
    extractor =
PatchExtractor(patch_size=extracted_patch_size,
    max_patches=N, random_state=0)
    patches = extractor.transform(img[np.newaxis])
    if scale != 1:
    patches = np.array([transform.resize(patch, patch_size)
    for patch in patches])
    return patches

negative_patches = np.vstack([extract_patches(im, 1000,
scale)
for im in images for scale in [0.5, 1.0, 2.0]])
Negative_patches.shape
```

Out[5]:

(30000, 62, 47)

We now have 30,000 suitable image patches which do not contain faces. Let's take a look at a few of them to get an idea of what they look like:

In [6]:

```
fig, ax = plt.subplots(6, 10)
for i, axi in enumerate(ax.flat):
axi.imshow(negative_patches[500 * i], cmap='gray')
axi.axis('off')
```

3. Third, from these training samples, extract HOG features.

```
from itertools import chain
X_train = np.array([feature.hog(im)
                    for im in chain(positive_patches,
                                    negative_patches)])
y_train = np.zeros(X_train.shape[0])
y_train[:positive_patches.shape[0]] = 1
X_train.shape
Out[8]:
(43233, 1215)
```

4. Train a linear SVM classifier on these samples.

SOME OTHER MACHINE LEARNING RESOURCES

The topic of machine learning is very diverse and vast. Therefore, it is impossible to bring it down to a few thousand words. However, if you are interested in machine learning, and you want to explore more into this amazing world, below are a few brilliant resources from where you can learn more.

MACHINE LEARNING IN PYTHON

1. The Scikit-Learn website: if you wish to learn some common-in-use machine learning algorithms, you can visit this website.

2. *SciPy, PyCon, and PyData tutorial videos.*

3. *Introduction to Machine Learning with Python* written by Andreas C. Mueller and Sara Guido.

4. *Python Machine Learning* by Sebastian Raschka.

GENERAL MACHINE LEARNING RESOURCES

1. Machine Learning taught by Andrew Ng (Coursera).

2. *Pattern Recognition and Machine Learning* by Christopher Bishop.

3. *Machine Learning*: A Probabilistic Perspective by Kevin Murphy.

CHAPTER 3

INTRODUCTION TO NUMPY

WHAT IS NUMPY?

In this chapter, we will look at some of the useful techniques for efficiently loading, storing and manipulating in-memory data in Python. The topic is vast because the sources from which data can be extracted are vast; it includes document collection, image collection, sound clips collection, or any other thing. Although, on the façade, the data is heterogenous, it will be taken fundamentally as arrays of numbers.

Let us take a quick example of digital images. They can be simply taken as two-dimensional arrays of numbers which denote pixel brightness across the area. Moreover, Sound clips can be taken as one-dimensional arrays of intensity vs time. Time, likewise, can be transformed into numerical representations in numerous ways (One way is binary digits signifying the frequency of some pair of words or words only).

Owing to this cause, good storage and manipulation of numerical arrays is the core of every process in data science. Now, there are two specialized tools that Python uses for handling these numerical arrays: the NumPy package, and the Pandas package. In this chapter we will go into the details of the NumPy package.

NumPy is the compact form for Numerical Python. It gives an effective interface to work on heavy data buffers. You may take NumPy as Python's ready-made list type, but its storage and data operation capabilities are much sounder, especially when the arrays become larger in size.

NumPy arrays form the core of nearly the entire ecosystem of data science tools in Python, so time spent learning to use NumPy effectively will be valuable no matter what aspect of data science interests you.

In chapter one, if you carefully follow the instructions of how to install the Anaconda stack, you would already have NumPy installed with you. However, if you want to do it all by yourself, then you may go on the website, http://www.numpy.org/ and follow the instructions given there.

Once you do, you can import NumPy and double-check the version:

In [1]:

import numpy

numpy.__version__

Out[1]:

'1.11.1'

For the pieces of the package discussed here, I'd recommend NumPy version 1.8 or later. By convention, you'll find that most people in the SciPy/PyData world will import NumPy using np as an alias:

In [2]:

import numpy as np

Use the interactive shell to try NumPy in the browser:

To try the examples in the browser:

1. Type code in the input cell and press

   Shift + Enter to execute

2. Or copy-paste the code, and click on

   the "Run" button in the toolbar

"""

The standard way to import NumPy:

import numpy as np

Create a 2-D array, set every second element in

some rows and find max per row:

x = np.arange(15, dtype=np.int64).reshape(3, 5)

x[1:, ::2] = -99

x

array([[0, 1, 2, 3, 4],

[-99, 6, -99, 8, -99],

```
#        [-99, 11, -99, 13, -99]])
```

```
x.max(axis=1)
```

```
# array([ 4,  8, 13])
```

```
# Generate normally distributed random numbers:
```

```
rng = np.random.default_rng()
```

```
samples = rng.normal(size=2500)
```

```
samples
```

SOME BASIC DATA TYPES IN NUMPY

Data storage and manipulation is fundamental to help understand effective data-driven science. In this section, you will learn how data arrays are taken care of in Python and how NumPy makes improvements on this.

Python users mostly prefer Python because of its easy-to-use feature of dynamic typing. If you look into other complicated languages like Java or C, you will notice how each variable is to be openly declared, however Python skips this. In C you might see a particular operation as given below:

```
/* C code */

int result = 0;

for(int i=0; i<100; i++){

    result += i;

}
```

In Python, on the other hand, the same operation can be written as:

```
# Python code
result = 0
for i in range(100):
    result += i
```

Observing these examples, you might notice the difference between C and Python; in the former, the data type of each variable is clearly demonstrated, whereas in the latter, the data types are inferred. By this, it is clear that we can allocate any kind of data to any kind of variable.

```
# Python code
```

```
x = 4
x = "four"
```

Notice, how the contents of x are changed from an integer to a string. If you do a similar thing in C, you will only make things more erroneous.

```
/* C code */
int x = 4;
x = "four"; // FAILS
```

This function or rather characteristic is what makes dynamically-typed languages like Python so convenient to use. Learning to operate this functioning is the cornerstone of learning how to efficiently analyze the data. However, one thing you should keep in mind is that Python variables also provide additional information about the data type.

A PYTHON INTEGER

Every Python implementation is written in C generally. Which means that any Python object is, in reality, a masked C structure, which does not only provide its value, but some other information too. For example, when we define integer x in $x=1000$, we do not consider x as just a 'raw' integer. X is actually an indicator to a compound structure of C which has many values. If we look through the Python 3.4 source code, we will come to know that the long type definition of integer looks like this.

```
struct _longobject {

    long ob_refcnt;

    PyTypeObject *ob_type;

    size_t ob_size;

    long ob_digit[1];
};
```

In python, integer storing is not an easy game as it is convenient in the compiled language process. Python integer is a pointer in a memory which consists of bytes which contain the value of integer. Moreover, information is additional in this python which provides assistance in active coding.

COMPUTATION ON NUMPY ARRAYS

NumPy array is a necessity of the python data science world. It provides a convenient interface in computation to the user. This array can work on both extremes, given if it is high speed or low speed. Through *vectorized operations* faster speeds are obtained.

SLOWNESS OF LOOPS

Any problem in the interpretation of python can result in a default, known as CPython. This is because of convenience in the interpretation of the language. These kinds of defaults are sought out with the help of **Py.Py** project, referring to the compilation in proper time. Some of the other projects are **Cython** and **Numba.** Each of them has their advantages as well as disadvantages but it is not wrong to say that these projects had passed the limit of their reach.

Operating smaller operations, leads to the slowness of Python. For instance, looping over arrays to work on the single value, makes the operation run at very low speed. Measuring time of operation for the code, especially in the bigger inputs, depicts a very sluggish response. For working efficiently compiled language is helpful but due to dynamic checkup for the proper functioning, it becomes slow.

Python data manipulation is nearly equivalent to the NumPy array operation. These are some of the classifications of NumPy array manipulations.

Attributes of arrays which refer to size and shape. Secondly, there comes an index *of arrays* which includes setting the values. Moreover; slicing, reshaping, reshaping and joining performs their respective functions.

NumPy's random number generator will be helpful in maintaining random array value whenever a different code is used.

Furthermore, these arrays consist of attributes. Some of these important attributes are *ndim, size, shape, dtype*. These all attributes perform their respective functions, for example, *nbytes* list total bytes of the array.

INTRODUCING UFUNCS

NumPy provides a user-friendly interface. *Vectorized operation* is the method of providing faster speed. This operation refers to the compiled layers under the operation of NumPy. These operations are performed through *ufuncs*. Its major function is to perform repeated operations in a short time on the given values of NumPy array. It is highly convenient to work with. They are not only restricted to the one-dimensional array but to the multi-dimensional arrays. Whenever we see arrays in larger size, we should be considering using this vectorization.

EXPLORING NumPY'S UFuncs

There are two types of ufuncs, *unary ufuncs* and *binary ufuncs* performing for the single input and double outputs respectively.

ARRAY ARITHMETIC

NumPy's ufuncs are easy to use as they make use of standard arithmetic operations. These include addition, subtraction, multiplication and division. These operations are acting like a cover to the particular function, for instance, + operation is the wrapper for the *add* function. We'll use NumPy's random number generator, which we will *seed* with a set value in order to ensure that the same random arrays are generated each time this code is run:

```
import numpy as np
np.random.seed(0)  # seed for reproducibility

x1 = np.random.randint(10, size=6)  # One-dimensional array
x2 = np.random.randint(10, size=(3, 4))  # Two-dimensional array
x3 = np.random.randint(10, size=(3, 4, 5))  # Three-dimensional array
```

Each array has attributes ndim (the number of dimensions), shape (the size of each dimension), and size (the total size of the array):

```
print("x3 ndim: ", x3.ndim)
print("x3 shape:", x3.shape)
print("x3 size: ", x3.size)
```

x3 ndim: 3
x3 shape: (3, 4, 5)
x3 size: 60

Another useful attribute is the dtype:

```
print("dtype:", x3.dtype)
```

dtype: int64

Other attributes include itemsize, which lists the size (in bytes) of each array element, and nbytes, which lists the total size (in bytes) of the array:

```
print("itemsize:", x3.itemsize, "bytes")
print("nbytes:", x3.nbytes, "bytes")
```

itemsize: 8 bytes
nbytes: 480 bytes

In general, we expect that nbytes is equal to itemsize times size.

The following table lists the arithmetic operators implemented in NumPy:

Operator	Equivalent ufunc	Description
+	np.add	Addition (e.g., $1 + 1 = 2$)
-	np.subtract	Subtraction (e.g., $3 - 2 = 1$)
-	np.negative	Unary negation (e.g., -2)
*	np.multiply	Multiplication (e.g., $2 * 3 = 6$)
/	np.divide	Division (e.g., $3 / 2 = 1.5$)
//	np.floor_divide	Floor division (e.g., $3 // 2 = 1$)
**	np.power	Exponentiation (e.g., $2 ** 3 = 8$)
%	np.mod	Modulus/remainder (e.g., $9 \% 4 = 1$)

ABSOLUTE VALUE

As NumPy's operator uses arithmetic operations, it also uses built-in absolute value functions.

TRIGONOMETRIC FUNCTIONS

NumPy performs important functions but the function of utmost importance is trigonometric functions. Machine precision is computed so as for the values which are zero should not be hitting an exact zero.

EXPONENTS AND LOGARITHMS

Another frequently used operation used in NumPy ufunc are the exponentials. Logarithms, inverse of the exponentials are also available. Moreover, base-2 and base-10 logarithms are also used.

SPECIALIZED UFUNCS

NumPy consists of other ufuncs, some of them are; hyperbolic trig functions, bitwise arithmetic, comparison operators, conversions from radians to degrees, rounding and remainders, and many more.

Submodule is another reliable source for the specialized ufuncs. If you are to compute obscure mathematical functions then the submodule method is of great importance.

ADVANCED UFUNC FEATURES

Many users cannot work by learning how to deal with different NumPy features so, some specialized features are outlined below:

SPECIFYING OUTPUT

Sizable calculations sometimes require specifying an array because using temporary arrays is hectic. So, we can write this computation directly into the main memory.

For instance, the value being computed is y[::2] = 2 ** x, this would result in the generating of a temporary array, detaining results of 2 ** x, pursued by the second operation for containing the value of y. But for the minute computations it is not necessary.

AGGREGATES

Some of the reliable aggregates are there to use. For example, reducing an array requires **reducing the ufunc** method as an operation. *Reduce* is constantly applied on the given operation, so as to single out the particular operation.

For the specified cases, there are specified NumPy functions to perform the results. For example,
np.sum, np.prod, np.cumsum, np.cumprod.

OUTER PRODUCTS

Using the output method, results of two inputs can be produced. Multiplication table is formed due to this:

x = np.arange(1, 6)

np.multiply.outer(x, x)

```
array([[ 1,  2,  3,  4,  5],
       [ 2,  4,  6,  8, 10],
       [ 3,  6,  9, 12, 15],
       [ 4,  8, 12, 16, 20],
       [ 5, 10, 15, 20, 25]])
```

To perform its function between dual arrays is ufunc remarkable ability, for instance operating between different sizes and shapes, known as *broadcasting*.

UFUNCS; LEARNING MORE

More information on this function can be found on the documentation's websites of

NumPy and SciPy.

Aggregations: Min, Max, and Everything In Between

When working with a heavy amount of data. To initiate, we make summary statistics of that data to make it precise. Most regularly used summary statistics are *mean* and *standard deviation*. There are some other methods like sum, product, median etc.

NumPy has some aggregate functions which are proved useful, when working on arrays.

Summing the Values in an Array

Python itself can compute summing of values but the problem is that compilation code is adopted in its operations, so comparatively NumPy array is swifter in its operation.

np.sum has relevance with multiple array dimensions but *sum* does not.

consider computing the sum of all values in an array. Python itself can do this using the built-in `sum` function:

In [1]:

```python
import numpy as np
```

In [2]:

```python
L = np.random.random(100)

sum(L)
```

Out[2]:

```
55.61209116604941
```

The syntax is quite similar to that of NumPy's `sum` function, and the result is the same in the simplest case:

```
np.sum(L)
```

```
55.612091166049424
```

However, because it executes the operation in compiled code, NumPy's version of the operation is computed much more quickly:

```
big_array = np.random.rand(1000000)
%timeit sum(big_array)
%timeit np.sum(big_array)


10 loops, best of 3: 104 ms per loop
1000 loops, best of 3: 442 µs per loop
```

Minimum and Maximum

Python has these functions of *min* and *max* which are already found in it. But again, NumPy has these functions in quicker version. Using the NumPy version of aggregates is favorable in dealing with NumPy arrays.

Python has built-in `min` and `max` functions, used to find the
minimum value and maximum value of any given array:

```
min(big_array), max(big_array)
```

```
(1.1717128136634614e-06, 0.9999976784968716)
```
NumPy's corresponding functions have similar syntax, and
again operate much more quickly:

```
np.min(big_array), np.max(big_array)
```

```
(1.1717128136634614e-06, 0.9999976784968716)
```

```
%timeit min(big_array)

%timeit np.min(big_array)
```

```
10 loops, best of 3: 82.3 ms per loop

1000 loops, best of 3: 497 µs per loop
```

For `min`, `max`, `sum`, and several other NumPy aggregates, a shorter syntax is to use methods of the array object itself:

In [8]:

```
print(big_array.min(), big_array.max(),
big_array.sum())
```

```
1.17171281366e-06 0.999997678497 499911.62819
```

Multi-dimensional aggregates

For instance, data is given in two-dimensional arrays. NumPy array aggregation will be applied on the complete array. Moreover, an aggregation function sets the particular axis along which aggregates are being calculated. The word used here regarding usage of specific axes refers to the dimension of arrays which are to be slumped.

One common type of aggregation operation is an aggregate along a row or column. Say you have some data stored in a two-dimensional array:

In [9]:

```
M = np.random.random((3, 4))

print(M)
```

```
[[ 0.8967576    0.03783739  0.75952519  0.06682827]

 [ 0.8354065    0.99196818  0.19544769  0.43447084]

 [ 0.66859307  0.15038721  0.37911423  0.6687194 ]]
```

By default, each NumPy aggregation function will return the aggregate over the entire array:

```
M.sum()
```

```
6.0850555667307118
```

Aggregation functions take an additional argument specifying the *axis* along which the aggregate is computed. For example, we can find the minimum value within each column by specifying `axis=0`:

```
M.min(axis=0)
```

```
array([ 0.66859307,   0.03783739,   0.19544769,
0.06682827])
```

The function returns four values, corresponding to the four columns of numbers.

Similarly, we can find the maximum value within each row:

```
M.max(axis=1)
```

```
array([ 0.8967576 ,  0.99196818,  0.6687194 ])
```

OTHER AGGREGATION FUNCTIONS

There are some of the other aggregate functions which are delivered to us through NumPy. Furthermore, NaN -safe functions perform by disregarding missed functions, which are pointed out through distinctive IEEE floating-
point NaN value.

The following table provides us a list of functional aggregates of NumPy.

Function Name	NaN-safe Version	Description
np.sum	np.nansum	Compute sum of elements

Function Name	NaN-safe Version	Description
np.prod	np.nanprod	Compute product of elements
np.mean	np.nanmean	Compute mean of elements
np.std	np.nanstd	Compute standard deviation
np.var	np.nanvar	Compute variance
np.min	np.nanmin	Find minimum value
np.max	np.nanmax	Find maximum value
np.argmin	np.nanargmin	Find index of minimum value
np.argmax	np.nanargmax	Find index of maximum value
np.median	np.nanmedian	Compute median of elements
np.percentile	np.nanpercentile	Compute rank-based statistics of elements
np.any	N/A	Evaluate whether any elements are true

Function Name	NaN-safe Version	Description
np.all	N/A	Evaluate whether all elements are true

Example: What is the Average Height of US Presidents?

Let's consider an example by taking into account heights of presidents of the US.

```
!head -4 data/president_heights.csv
order,name,height(cm)
1,George Washington,189
2,John Adams,170
3,Thomas Jefferson,189
```

As we know NumPy arrays are useful when summary statistics of data is being surveyed.

```
import pandas as pd
data = pd.read_csv('data/president_heights.csv')
heights = np.array(data['height(cm)'])
print(heights)
```

[189 170 189 163 183 171 185 168 173 183 173 173 175 178 183
193 178 173
 174 183 183 168 170 178 182 180 183 178 182 188 175 179 183
193 182 183
 177 185 188 188 182 185]

With the help of this data, we are capable of computing summary statistics of data.

```
print("Mean height:      ", heights.mean())
print("Standard deviation:", heights.std())
print("Minimum height:   ", heights.min())
print("Maximum height:   ", heights.max())
Mean height:      179.738095238
Standard deviation: 6.93184344275
Minimum height:    163
Maximum height:    193
```

This aggregation operation will help us to summarize into a single array, this helps us to understand distribution of values. Quantiles can also be computed:

```
print("25th percentile:  ", np.percentile(heights, 25))
print("Median:           ", np.median(heights))
print("75th percentile:  ", np.percentile(heights, 75))
```

25th percentile: 174.25

Median: 182.0

75th percentile: 183.0

Median height can be seen which is 182cm. Discernible representation is sometimes more preferable.


```
%matplotlib inline
import matplotlib.pyplot as plt
import seaborn; seaborn.set()  # set plot style
```

```
plt.hist(heights)
plt.title('Height Distribution of US Presidents')
plt.xlabel('height (cm)')
plt.ylabel('number');
```

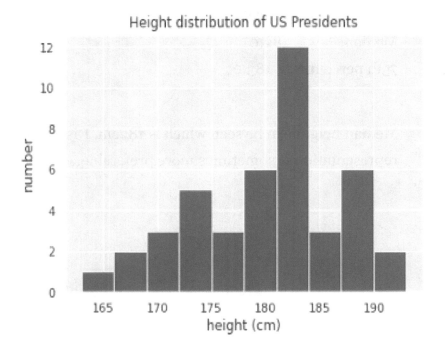

Height distribution of US Presidents

COMPUTATION ARRAYS: BROADCASTING

Previously, we have learned NumPy's vectorization operations. Now another method to study vectorization operations is NumPy's *broadcasting* functionality. It is the number of instructions for algebraic operations.

INTRODUCING BROADCASTING

These binary ufuncs can be applied on multi-size arrays. For instance, a scalar can be added, that is, a zero- dimensional array. This operation can be interpreted as replicating values and adding the resulting solution. A real advantage of this operation is having a replica` as a mental model and not the real one. Furthermore, these functions can be implemented on the higher-dimensional arrays. Result of adding one-dimensional array with the two-dimensional array as, stretching of one-dimensional array value across the second-dimensional array, in order to make the values equal.

In more confusing cases, broadcasting of both arrays is involved. As we have stretched the values to match them in previous cases, here we have stretched both values to match the regular values and the resulting answer is a two-dimensional array.

Rules of Broadcasting

Broadcasting in NumPy's operations follows some set of rules which are as follow:

Rule 1: When the two dimension numbers are not similar, the one with lesser number of dimensions is covered by the dimension which is superior to it.

Rule 2: Difference in the shape of both dimensions, the array matching the shape of 1 in that dimension is stretched to equal the shapes.

Rule 3: Difference in sizes of dimensions, elevates an error.

BROADCASTING EXAMPLE

Consider an example where the two arrays are not well matched.

M = np.ones((3, 2))
a = np.arange(3)

In the following example, matrix M is switched. Arrays shapes are as follow:

- M.shape = (3, 2)
- a.shape = (3,)

According to rule 1, padding of shape a with ones takes place as these dimensions differ in numbers.

- M.shape -> (3, 2)
- a.shape -> (1, 3)

Applying rule 2, will help us stretch dimension a to match it to M.

- M.shape -> (3, 2)
- a.shape -> (3, 3)

Finally, rule 3, which depicts both are not equal.

Now, bear this in mind that we try to make both dimensions compatible by applying rule 1. But this is not how broadcasting of NumPy's operation works. These rules can be of help in many cases but it can raise serious confusions.

As we have been, concentrating on the + operator, broadcasting rules can be implemented on any binary ufuncs.

Broadcasting in Practice

We will see here how these examples can be helpful:

CENTERING AN ARRAY

Broadcasting enhances the capability of NumPy's users by eliminating the need of writing slow Python loops. One commonly known example of this is centering of an array of data.

Mean aggregate can be used to operate on the mean of each figure. Then, centering an array is helped by subtracting the mean. For ensuring the correct result, we can verify that the centered array has near zero mean.

Plotting a two-dimensional function

Exhibiting images based on the two-dimensional functions, is one of broadcasting's main advantages. For instance, if we want to define the function **z=f(x+y),** we can use broadcasting to operate this function across the grid.

COMPARISONS, MASKS AND BOOLEAN LOGIC

By this time, you must be familiar with the basic concepts in NumPy arrays. Now, let us dig into the use of Boolean masks to analyze and change the values within NumPy arrays. When you wish to extract, enhance, count or manipulate values within an array on some specific standard, you can make use of the technique of masking. In NumPy, the most effective way to achieve tasks like counting all values bigger than a specific value is to use Boolean masking.

You might be familiar with the fact that NumPy's ufuncs can replace loops to do quick element-wise arithmetic operations on arrays. Other than arithmetic operations, NumPy ufuncs can also perform element-wise comparison over arrays. Also, results can be manipulated to get answers to our questions. Let us dig into some basic tools in NumPy that use masking to quickly and effectively answer our questions.

Before, we have just focused on element-wise arithmetic operators by using +, -, *, /. Comparison operators implemented by NumPy are < (less than) and > (greater than). The end result that we get of these comparison operators is always an array with a Boolean data type.

WORKING WITH A BOOLEAN ARRAY

There are various useful operations one can perform using a Boolean array. Let us take an example of x, a two-dimensional array.

In [14]:
print(x)

[[5 0 3 3]
 [7 9 3 5]
 [2 4 7 6]]

When counting entries, the best way to count True entries in a Boolean array is to use np.count_nonzero . Sum() is useful because like all other NumPy aggregation functions, the addition can be performed along rows or columns as well. Moreover, if we are interested in checking if all of the values are true or not, we can use np.any or np.all

FANCY INDEXING

This type of indexing is a simpler way for array indexing, which helps us in altering complex subsets of array's values. It is concerned with array indices rather than single scalar.

EXPLORING FANCY INDEXING

As discussed above, it is related to passing of array indices which is helpful in approaching multiple array elements in one go. When working with fancy indexes, the shape of the result is the shape of index arrays and not of the array being indexed.

This type of indexing assists us in multiple dimensions. For instance, in an array, consider standard indexing which will refer its first index to the row and second index to the column. On the other hand, pairing of indices in fancy indexing is accompanied with all the broadcasting rules as learned before. So, combining these column vectors and row vector indices, we get a two-dimensional result.

Always bear in mind that with fancy indexing, the result value shows the broadcasted shape of indices and not the shape of the array being indexed.

For example, consider the following array:

In [1]:

```
import numpy as np

rand = np.random.RandomState(42)


x = rand.randint(100, size=10)

print(x)
```

```
[51 92 14 71 60 20 82 86 74 74]
```

Suppose we want to access three different elements. We could do it like this:

```
[x[3], x[7], x[2]]
```

```
[71, 86, 14]
```

Alternatively, we can pass a single list or array of indices to obtain the same result:

```
ind = [3, 7, 4]

x[ind]
```

```
array([71, 86, 60])
```

When using fancy indexing, the shape of the result reflects the shape of the *index arrays* rather than the shape of the *array being indexed*:

```
ind = np.array([[3, 7],
                [4, 5]])

x[ind]
```

```
array([[71, 86],

       [60, 20]])
```

Fancy indexing also works in multiple dimensions. Consider the following array:

```
X = np.arange(12).reshape((3, 4))

X
```

```
array([[ 0,   1,   2,   3],

       [ 4,   5,   6,   7],

       [ 8,   9,  10,  11]])
```

Like with standard indexing, the first index refers to the row, and the second to the column:

```
row = np.array([0, 1, 2])

col = np.array([2, 1, 3])
```

```
X[row, col]
```

```
array([ 2,   5,  11])
```

Notice that the first value in the result is `x[0, 2]`, the second is `x[1, 1]`, and the third is `x[2, 3]`. The pairing of indices in fancy indexing follows all the broadcasting rules that were mentioned in Computation on Arrays: Broadcasting. So, for example, if we combine a column vector and a row vector within the indices, we get a two-dimensional result:

```
X[row[:, np.newaxis], col]
```

```
array([[ 2,   1,   3],
       [ 6,   5,   7],
       [10,   9,  11]])
```

Here, each row value is matched with each column vector, exactly as we saw in broadcasting of arithmetic operations. For example:

```
row[:, np.newaxis] * col
```

```
array([[0, 0, 0],
       [2, 1, 3],
       [4, 2, 6]])
```

COMBINED INDEXING

To influence our operations, we can consider combining fancy indexing with other indexing schemes. As collaboration of fancy indexing with simple indices. Likewise, combining fancy indexes with slicing and masking. Cooperation of all these functions, leads us to deal with fast and elastic operations.

For even more powerful operations, fancy indexing can be combined with the other indexing schemes we've seen:

```
print(X)
```

```
[[ 0  1  2  3]
 [ 4  5  6  7]
 [ 8  9 10 11]]
```

We can combine fancy and simple indices:

In [10]:

```
X[2, [2, 0, 1]]
```

Out[10]:

```
array([10,  8,  9])
```

We can also combine fancy indexing with slicing:

In [11]:

```
X[1:, [2, 0, 1]]
```

Out[11]:

```
array([[ 6,  4,  5],
       [10,  8,  9]])
```

And we can combine fancy indexing with masking:

In [12]:

```
mask = np.array([1, 0, 1, 0], dtype=bool)

X[row[:, np.newaxis], mask]
```

Out[12]:

103

```
array([[ 0,   2],

       [ 4,   6],

       [ 8,  10]])
```

Modifying Values with Fancy Indexing

Altering parts of an array is of significance when working with fancy indexing. Let's consider an array of indices in which we set the corresponding items, this can be worked out with any assignment operator. Similar indices within these operations often causes unimaginable results.

It works sometimes against our expectations. For instance,

i = [2, 3, 3, 4, 4, 4]
x[i] += 1
x

Out[21]:
array([6., 0., 1., 1., 1., 0., 0., 0., 0., 0.])

In this array, we expect to have x[3] to have value 2, and x[4] to have value 4. But that is not the case. This is because x[i] += 1 is taken as a shorthand of x[i] = x[i] + 1. x[i] + 1 is assessed and the solution is allocated to the indices in x. Evaluation is not what happens multiple times but the assignment which leads to unreasonable results. So, if you require another behavior where operation is repeated, we can utilize the at( ) method of ufuncs. The at( ) method holds significance when it does an in-place application of the given operator at the particular indices with some particular values. Another type of method which is similar in nature to it is reduceat( ), which can be further studied in NumPy documentation.

BINNING OF DATA

Binning data to make histogram by hand is another advantage which can be applied using these ideas. Let's consider we have 1,000 values, and we want to fix them within appropriate array bins. This can be helped with the usage of ufuncs.

Plotting histogram is plotted with help of matplotlib, which provides *plt.hist( )* routine. It uses the function *np.histogram* which performs a similar operation to one we did before.

One-line algorithm is way faster than the optimized algorithm in NumPy. NumPy's algorithm works efficiently when we see *np.histogram* source code, especially when we have a larger number of data points. This type of algorithm is not always the best choice for smaller data sets.

SORTING ARRAYS

Have you ever heard about insertion sorts, selection sorts, merge sorts, quick sorts, or bubble sorts? I am sure most of you got acquainted with this term while doing an introductory computer science course. These terms are nothing but mere means to achieve the task of sorting the values in a list or array.

FAST SORTING IN NUMPY: *np.sort* AND *np.argsort*

NumPy's *np.sort* function is much more effective and useful for our purposes than the built-in sort and *sorted* function in Python. *np.sort* uses *quicksort* algorithm in most of the applications, and rarely are *mergesort* and *heapsort* used as they are not its default algorithm.

If you wish to not alter the input and at the same time, return a sorted version of the array, you may use np.sort:

In [5]:
```
x = np.array([2, 1, 4, 3, 5])
np.sort(x)
```

Out[5]:
```
array([1, 2, 3, 4, 5])
```

However, if you wish to sort the array in-place, *sort* method of arrays is more convenient

In [6]:

```
x.sort()
print(x)
```
[1 2 3 4 5]

Argsort is another function which is used to return the *indices* of the sorted elements.

In [7]:
```
x = np.array([2, 1, 4, 3, 5])
i = np.argsort(x)
print(i)
```
[1 0 3 2 4]

NumPy's sorting algorithm also has the feature of sorting along specific rows or columns of a multidimensional array by making use of the axis argument.

PARTITIONING: PARTIAL SORTS

You might have noticed that often you desire to find the k smallest values in the arrays, instead of sorting the whole array, but you do not know how to do it. *Np.partition* function of NumPy is the answer to this. *Np.partition* uses an array and any number *K*. The result you get is a new array with the smallest *K* values which are visible on the left-hand side of the partition, whereas the remaining values are shown on the right in a random order.

In [12]:
x = np.array([7, 2, 3, 1, 6, 5, 4])
np.partition(x, 3)

Out[12]:
array([2, 1, 3, 4, 6, 5, 7])

You can see from the above example, that the first three values in the resulting array are the smallest values, and the rest of the array positions have the remaining values. Also, within the partitions, the elements are arranged in an arbitrary order.

Not only this, we can also perform partition along an arbitrary axis with a multidimensional array. For example,
In [13]:

np.partition(X, 2, axis=1)

Out[13]:
array([[3, 4, 6, 7, 6, 9],
       [2, 3, 4, 7, 6, 7],
       [1, 2, 4, 5, 7, 7],
       [0, 1, 4, 5, 9, 5]])

As you can see, in the resulting array, the first two slots in each row have the smallest values from that row; the left-over values are contained by the remaining slots.

STRUCTURED DATA: NUMPY'S STRUCTURED ARRAY

Demonstration of data with array values is sometimes not suitable. Instead, we can work with heterogeneous array values to represent our data as it will prove useful in most of the circumstances because of its adaptable storage.

Consider different categories of data on the number of people, for instance; weight, height, name, age. To utilize them in the python program we will store these values. They can be stored in three arrays, but it will be more ungraceful. So, we would prefer a single array for storing the data. NumPy is most likely to use structured arrays to perform this function more efficiently.

```
# Use a compound data type for structured arrays
data = np.zeros(4, dtype={'names':('name', 'age', 'weight'),
                'formats':('U10', 'i4', 'f8')})
print(data.dtype)
[('name', '<U10'), ('age', '<i4'), ('weight', '<f8')]
```

'U10' refers to "Unicode string of maximum length 10," 'i4' refers to "4-byte (i.e., 32 bit) integer," and 'f8' refers to "8-byte (i.e., 64 bit) float."

When a vacant container array is obtained, we can fill out the array with our values.

```
data['name'] = name
data['age'] = age
data['weight'] = weight
print(data)
[('Alice', 25, 55.0) ('Bob', 45, 85.5) ('Cathy', 37, 68.0)
 ('Doug', 19, 61.5)]
```
So according to our wish, we have obtained the data values in a single array which is more flexible and suitable. We can indicate the values either by name or index, which is another convenience with structured arrays. Moreover, Boolean masking is helpful in performing sophisticated operations like filtering.

Concludingly, complicated arrays are more likely to be performed with the help of Pandas package.

CREATING STRUCTURED ARRAYS

Structuring arrays can be used particularly for variable functions. Numerical types are set out through Python types. Similarly, compound types are identified as a list of tuples and if the names of types are of no concern to you, you can set out the types alone in comma-separated string. The minimized format codes can be a bit confusing but are assembled on basic principles. First character specifies the sequence of potent bits. The characters next to them refer to the type of data and the final characters show the size of objects in bytes.

MORE ADVANCED COMPOUND TYPES

More advanced compound types can be elaborated. For instance, we can build types where every single element consists of an array. Here, we built a data type with a mat component.

We don't use multi-dimensional arrays in this case because of the reason that NumPy *dtype* instantly links to C structure definition which helps in connecting to the buffer (containing the array content) immediately with a proper written C program. Structures are quite useful when working on a Python interface to a legacy C.

CHAPTER 4

INTRODUCTIONS TO VISUALIZATIONS WITH MATPLOTLIB

Matplotlib is multitasking data visualization which was originated by John Hunter in 2002. Its value was elevated when it was used as the plotting package of choice of the Space telescope Science Institute, which gave support to matplotlib financially and assisted in magnifying its capabilities.

Matplotlib ability to perform well with operating systems. It adds support to hundreds of backends and output types, which ultimately means that without worry we can use any operating system or which output is of concern to you. Everything- to-everyone approach is the biggest advantage of Matplotlib. This approach has led to a vast user base, which ultimately leads to an active developer base.

However, Matplotlib has started losing its pace. Instead of interface and Matplotlib, ggplot and ggvis in the R language, outclass the Matplotlib data visualization. Still, Matplotlib enjoys great strength as a well-tested, cross-platform graphics engine. Newer versions of Matplotlib assist us to set up new global plotting styles. People have been developing packages built on dominant internals to run Matplotlib through cleaner, modern APIs. Pandas are also of assistance to Matplotlib's API. So, it can be concluded that Matplotlib is of great significance in data visualization.

GENERAL MATPLOTLIB TIPS

Here are some tips you should know while performing visualization with Matplotlib.

IMPORTING MATPLOTLIB

There are some abbreviations for Matplotlib imports which are known as standard shorthand. For instance, we have learned *np* as a shorthand for NumPy.

We use the np shorthand for NumPy and the pd shorthand for Pandas, we will utilize some standard shorthands for Matplotlib imports:

In[1]:

```
import matplotlib as mpl
```

```
import matplotlib.pyplot as plt
```

The plt will be the commonly used interface in this chapter.

SETTING STYLES

For pointing out relevant aesthetic styles for our figures, we will use *plt.style* directive. To make a certain classic Matplotlib style, use *classic.style* directive. Mind that, style sheets are operated through Matplotlib version 1.5, and using the older version of Matplotlib will only present the default style to you.

We will set the classic style, which makes sure that the plots we create use the classic Matplotlib style:

In[2]:

```
plt.style.use('classic')
```

SHOW() OR NO SHOW()? HOW TO DISPLAY YOUR PLOTS

Your context matters whenever we are citing Matplotlib plots. Its significance enlightens when it is used distinctly. Roughly, there are three pertinent contexts at hand using Matplotlib in script, in IPython terminal or in IPython notebook.

PLOTTING FROM A SCRIPT

Function *plt.show( )* will be at your service when using Matplotlib in script. The *plt.show( )* proceeds with an event loop and regards every current active figure object. Then it accesses interactive windows that present your respective figure.

Mostly *plt.show( )* works under the cover. It is an extensive type of operation, which has to collaborate with your interactive graphical backend. Moreover, it is very flexible as it varies not only from system to system but also from installation to installation.

For example, you may have a file called *myplot.py* containing the following:

```
# ------- file: myplot.py ------
import matplotlib.pyplot as plt
import numpy as np
x = np.linspace(0, 10, 100)
plt.plot(x, np.sin(x))
plt.plot(x, np.cos(x))
plt.show()
```

You can then run this script from the command-line prompt, which will result in a window opening with your figure displayed:

$ python myplot.py

The plt.show() command does a lot under the hood, as it must interact with your system's interactive graphical backend. The details of this operation can vary considerably from system to system and even installation to installation, but Matplotlib does its best to hide all these details from you.

Remember to always use *plt.show ( )* only once per Python session, because multiple shows can often lead to uncertain backend-dependent behavior.

PLOTTING FROM AN IPYTHON SHELL

It is a very interactive type of collaboration between Matplotlib and IPython shell. For this, using a particular Matplotlib code is required. For initiating this mode, use *%matplotlib* magic command after starting *ipython*. Here, any *plt* will make a figure window to open and following commands will be used for updating the plot. However, some changes will require different types of commands. For instance, for an update plt.draw( ) command is of significance.

To use this mode, you can enable the %matplotlib magic command after starting ipython:

In [1]:

%matplotlib

Using matplotlib backend: TkAgg

In [2]: import matplotlib.pyplot as plt

At this point, any plt plot command will generate a figure window to open, and further commands can be run to update the plot. Some modifications will not draw automatically; to force an update, use plt.draw(). Utilizing plt.show() in Matplotlib mode is not required.

PLOTTING FROM AN IPYTHON NOTEBOOK

IPython notebook is an associative type of browser that integrates narrative, code, graphics, HTML elements into one workable document. Plotting in the IPython notebook is assisted through the%matplotlib command. Furthermore, you have a choice to enclose graphics straight into the notebook.

%matplolib notebook and %matplotlib inline leads to setting graphics and static images of your plot in notebook respectively. *%matplotlib* inline will be commonly used in this section.

After running this command, any of the respective cells in the notebook, generating a plot will endorse a PNG image of the resulting graphic.

Plotting interactively within an IPython notebook can be done with the %matplotlib command, and works in a similar way to the IPython shell. In the IPython notebook, you also have the option of embedding graphics directly in the notebook, with two possible options:

- %matplotlib notebook will lead to *interactive* plots embedded within the notebook
- %matplotlib inline will lead to *static* images of your plot embedded in the notebook

For this book, we will generally opt for %matplotlib inline:
In[3]:
%matplotlib inline

After you run this command (it needs to be done only once per kernel/session), any cell within the notebook that creates a plot will embed a PNG image of the resulting graphic:

In[4]:

import numpy as np

```
x = np.linspace(0, 10, 100)
fig = plt.figure()
plt.plot(x, np.sin(x), '-')
plt.plot(x, np.cos(x), '--');
```

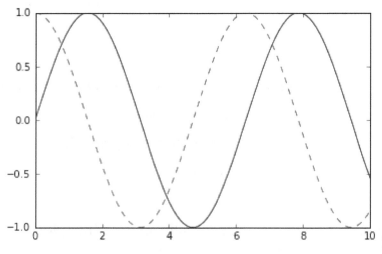

Figure 4-

1. Basic plotting example

SAVING FIGURES TO LIFE

Preserving figures in the broad category of formats is another advantage of Matplotlib. So, for saving a figure, you can use the command *savefig( )*.

File format is referred from the extension of filename in savefig( ) command. Different types of file format are accessible relying on the backends you have installed.

For example, to save the previous figure as a PNG file, you can run this:

In[5]:

```
fig.savefig('my_figure.png')
```

We now have a file called *my_figure.png* in the current working directory:

In[6]:

```
!ls -lh my_figure.png
-rw-r--r-- 1 jakevdp staff 16K Aug 11 10:59 my_figure.png
```

To confirm that it contains what we think it contains, let's use the IPython Image object to display the contents of this file:

In[7]:

```
 from IPython.display import Image
Image('my_figure.png')
```

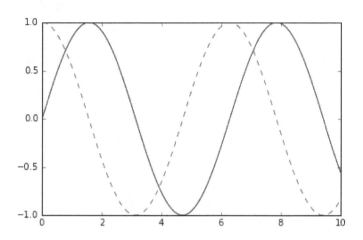

Figure 4-2. PNG rendering of the basic plot

In savefig(), the file format is inferred from the extension of the given filename. Depending on what backends you have installed, many different file formats are available. You can find the list of supported file types for your system by using the following method of the figure canvas object:

In[8]:
fig.canvas.get_supported_filetypes()
Out[8]:
{'eps': 'Encapsulated Postscript',
 'jpeg': 'Joint Photographic Experts Group',
 'jpg': 'Joint Photographic Experts Group',
    'pdf': 'Portable Document Format',

'pgf': 'PGF code for LaTeX',

'png': 'Portable Network Graphics',

'ps': 'Postscript',

'raw': 'Raw RGBA bitmap',

'rgba': 'Raw RGBA bitmap',

'svg': 'Scalable Vector Graphics',

'svgz': 'Scalable Vector Graphics',

'tif': 'Tagged Image File Format',

'tiff': 'Tagged Image File Format'}

SIMPLE LINE PLOTS

Previously we have learned basic data visualization. In this section, we will discuss the simplest plots. One of the simplest plots is, visualization of a single function $y=f(x)$. So. We will study how simple plots are being created.

Matplotlib plots are formed by the help of figures and axes. IN matplotlib, *figure* can be considered as a single holder of all the items which represents axes, graphics, texts and tables. On the other hand, *axes* is like an enclosing box, which borders all the plots needed for visualization.

fig will be used for figures instance and *ax* will be used for axes instance.

What we can use to create figures and axes is *pylab interface*.

ADJUSTING THE PLOT: LINE COLORS AND STYLES

Settings regarding the plot will be initiated through the control of line colors and styles. The *plt.plot ( )* is of assistance here. Likewise, *color* and *linestyle* can be used for adjusting colors and line style. Both of these can be used in a combination which turns it into a single non-keyword argument to the *plt.plot ( )* function.

ADJUSTING THE PLOT: AXES LIMITS

Selecting default axis limits for your plot is a particular job done by Matplolib. But sometimes it is not helpful and a better control is preferred. Most common types of methods used for specifying axes limits are plt.xlim() and plt.ylim().

The plt.axis( ) method is used for setting x and y axis limits in a very convenient way. It further assists in securing the borders around your current plot.

Moreover, equal aspect ratio is another quality.

LABELING PLOTS

Labeling of plots will be discussed briefly in this section.

Titles and axis tables are the simplest of all labels, there are some known methods which are of ultimate importance here.

For appropriate position, size and style of these labels, optional arguments are used.

Plot legend is to be preferred when multiple lines in single axes are being encountered. It will help in labeling each line. The quick way for producing this legend is using plt.legend( ).

ASIDE: MATPLOTLIB GOTCHAS

While many plt functions are directly interpreted into axes methods, this is not preferred in all cases. Some commands do need some modifications. For instance, when talking about functions to set limits or labels. For the conversion between MATLAB-style functions and object-oriented methods, some changes are needed, from which few are shown below:

- plt.xlabel() → ax.set_xlabel()

- plt.ylabel() → ax.set_ylabel()

In object-oriented interface to plotting, it is more appropriate to use ax.set( ) method. It is because this method assists in setting out all properties at once rather than operating on each one individually.

HISTOGRAMS, BINNINGS AND DENSITY

The famous hist() function provides you with many options to finetune the calculations as well as the display. If you want to have a look at a customized histogram, there is an example below:

```
plt.hist(data, bins=30, normed=True, alpha=0.5,
    histtype='stepfilled', color='steelblue',
    edgecolor='none');
```

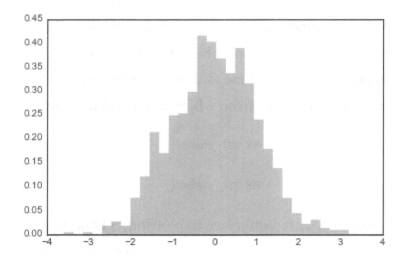

The plt.hist docstring has more information on other customization options available. I find this combination of histtype='stepfilled' along with some transparency alpha to be very useful when comparing histograms of several distributions:

In [4]:

```
x1 = np.random.normal(0, 0.8, 1000)
x2 = np.random.normal(-2, 1, 1000)
x3 = np.random.normal(3, 2, 1000)

kwargs = dict(histtype='stepfilled', alpha=0.3, normed=True,
bins=40)

plt.hist(x1, **kwargs)
plt.hist(x2, **kwargs)
plt.hist(x3, **kwargs);
```

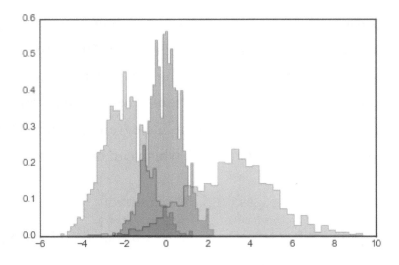

If you would like to simply compute the histogram (that is, count the number of points in a given bin) and not display it, the np.histogram() function is available:

In [5]:

125

```
counts, bin_edges = np.histogram(data, bins=5)
print(counts)
```
[12 190 468 301 29]

TWO-DIMENSIONAL HISTOGRAMS AND BINNING

Designing a histogram in two-dimensions is also possible by dividing points into two-dimensional bins. We will initiate the process by elaborating some data.

TWO-DIMENSIONAL HISTOGRAM

One easy way to go for creating a two-dimensional histogram, is to use *plt.hist2d* function of Matplotlib. These functions consist of additional points to fine-tune the plot and for binning. Moreover, these functions have their equivalents. Like, plt.hist has a parallel in np.histogram and plt.histo2d has its parallel in np.histogram2d, which can be used as:

```
counts, xedges, yedges = np.histogram2d(x, y, bins=30)
```

The matplotlib function np.histogram is of significance when binning in dimensions higher than two is needed.

PLT.HEXBIN: HEXAGONAL BINNINGS

Patches of squares along the axes are made when a two-dimensional hexagon is created. Matplotlib uses the function plt.hexbin, which represents a two-dimensional dataset binned into the patches of hexagons.

This function consists of several fascinating points which includes particularizing the weight of each point and altering the output in each bin to any NumPy aggregate.

KERNEL DENSITY ESTIMATION

Another simple method to consider densities in multiple dimensions is kernel density estimation (KDE). KDE is a method to "smear out" different points in space and then accumulate the result to get a smooth function. Scipy.stats package is a famous example of simple and fast KDE implementation. Let us look at a simple example of employing KDE on the data given below:

In [10]:
```python
from scipy.stats import gaussian_kde

# fit an array of size [Ndim, Nsamples]
data = np.vstack([x, y])
kde = gaussian_kde(data)

# evaluate on a regular grid
xgrid = np.linspace(-3.5, 3.5, 40)
ygrid = np.linspace(-6, 6, 40)
Xgrid, Ygrid = np.meshgrid(xgrid, ygrid)
Z = kde.evaluate(np.vstack([Xgrid.ravel(), Ygrid.ravel()]))

# Plot the result as an image
```

```
plt.imshow(Z.reshape(Xgrid.shape),
    origin='lower', aspect='auto',
    extent=[-3.5, 3.5, -6, 6],
    cmap='Blues')
cb = plt.colorbar()
cb.set_label("density")
```

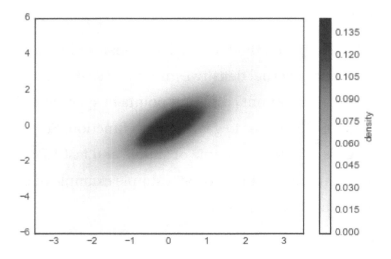

KDE has a smoothing length that quite efficiently slides the knob between detail and smoothness.

CUSTOMIZING PLOT LEGENDS

Plot legends are there to allocate some appropriate explanation to the visualization. Here we will learn simple legends techniques and how to adapt it within the technology of Matplotlib.

Simple legend will be adopted with the help of plt.legend( ) command, which spontaneously generates a legend for any labeled plot elements.

For adapting this legend, some methods which are of significance are; stating the location and turning of the frame.

Command nco1 is helpful in identifying the number of columns in the legend.

ax.legend(frameon=**False**, loc='lower center', ncol=2)
fig

Out[5]:

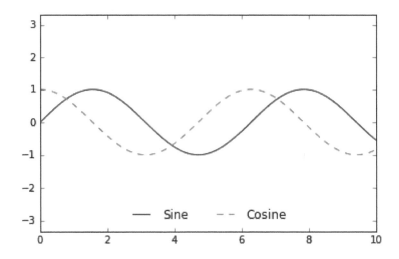

A round box known as fancybox is used for altering transparency and padding of the text.

CHOOSING ELEMENTS FOR THE LEGENDS

We can also fine-tune those elements and labels which are presented in the legends by the help of objects yielded by plot commands. The plt.plot( ) command is needed for generating a collection of lines at once and gives back the generated line instances. Driving them to plt.legend( ) will notify it which one to pick out, alongside the labels we like to particularize.

y = np.sin(x[:, np.newaxis] + np.pi * np.arange(0, 2, 0.5))
lines = plt.plot(x, y)

 # lines is a list of plt.Line2D instances
plt.legend(lines[:2], ['first', 'second']);

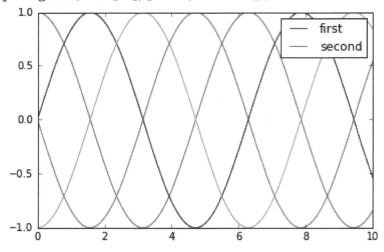

Using the first method is more suitable according to my preference, implementing labels to the plot elements you like to present on the legend.

LEGEND FOR SIZE OF POINTS

Occasionally the legend defaults are not adequate for the visualization. With the assistance of the size of points, you mark out particular characteristics of the data, and wish to create a legend through it. A legend is needed to set the scale for the size of points, and this will be achieved by plotting some labeled data.

There is a dire need to plot that certain shape which you want to represent because the legend will identify an object which is on the plot. If the particular object does not show up on the plot, all we need to do is to imitate them by plotting empty lists. By plotting these empty lists, we generate labeled plot objects which are chosen by the legend. This technique is helpful in creating enlightened visualizations.

For dealing with geographic data, a suitable tool to use is Matplotlib's Basemap addon toolkit.

MULTIPLE LEGENDS

While creating a plot, it is likely to add multiple legends to the same axes. Regrettably, Matplotlib does not give access to these functions easily. Standard legend interface is used only for single legends to create the whole plot. If you wish to generate a second legend with the help of plt.legend( ) and ax.legend( ), it will overthrow the first one with ease. By generating a new legend artist from the very start, will help you get around this, and after it, using ax.add_artist( ) command to dynamically add the second artist to the plot.

CUSTOMIZING COLORBARS

Plot legends recognize the irregular labels of discrete points. For regular labels established on color of paints, lines or regions, a labeled colorbar is all you need. In Matplotlib, a colorbar is a disparate axis which can give you a key to the meaning of colors in the plot.

If you wish to set out the colormap, cmap argument is applied on the plotting function which is creating the visualization.

plt.imshow(I, cmap='gray');

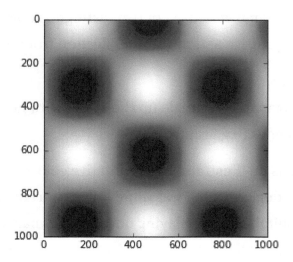

All the obtainable colormaps are in plt.cm namespace. Picking the appropriate colormap is just the initial step.

CHOOSING THE COLORMAP

Comprehensive study of colormap is beyond the range of this book, but for giving a light reading to it, see the article "Ten Simple Rules for Better Figures". Also, Matplotlib give some interesting information about it in online documentations.

It can be broadly divided into three categories:

Sequential colormaps: It consists of continuous patterns of colors (e.g., binary)

Divergent colormaps: It consist of two distinguishable colors, which refers to positive and negative deflection from mean (e.g., RdBu)

Qualitative colormaps: It mingle up the colors with no particular sequence (e.g., rainbow)

A jet colormap is an illustration of qualitative colormaps. It was stated as a default which was quite unlucky, as qualitative maps are not suitable for displaying quantitative maps. Moreover, these qualitative colormaps are at disadvantage when uniform progression in brightness is required.

view_colormap('jet')

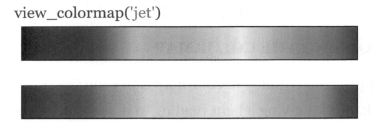

In this grayscale image, bright stripes are displayed as an uneven stripe. This uneven brightness will lead to creation of the eye to the specific parts of the color range, which marks the insignificant parts of the dataset. So, its better to go for viridis colormap which is specially created for the purpose of even brightness variation across the range.

Sometimes, when deviations from positive and negative values are required to be presented, they are backed up through the function of RdBu.

There are a variety of colormaps found on the Matplotlib, you can use IPython to survey the plt.cm submodule.

COLOR LIMITS AND EXTENSIONS

Matplotlib gives you a wide range of colorbar customization. Colorbar has some fascinating adaptiveness linked to it. For instance, color limits can be narrowed down.

```
# make noise in 1% of the image pixels
speckles = (np.random.random(I.shape) < 0.01)
I[speckles] = np.random.normal(0, 3,
np.count_nonzero(speckles))

plt.figure(figsize=(10, 3.5))

plt.subplot(1, 2, 1)
plt.imshow(I, cmap='RdBu')
plt.colorbar()

plt.subplot(1, 2, 2)
plt.imshow(I, cmap='RdBu')
plt.colorbar(extend='both')
plt.clim(-1, 1);
```

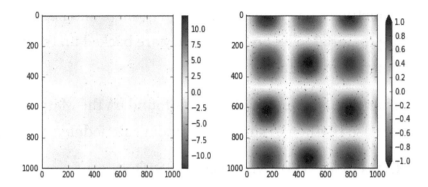

Remember that in the left panel, the default color limits answers to the noisy pixels and the patterns from which we are concerned are entirely washed-out. On the other hand, in the right panel, we can set the color limits optionally and to identify values we can simply extend them as they are not at the required limit level. Resulting solution is much more significant visualization of our data.

DISCRETE COLOR BARS

Colormaps as discussed above are continuous, but we will be requiring discrete values on some occasions. One easy method which will assist us on these occasions is plt.cm.get_cmap( ) function, and progress the name to the appropriate colormap with the number of required bins:

plt.imshow(I, cmap=plt.cm.get_cmap('Blues', 6))
plt.colorbar()

136

plt.clim(-1, 1);

The discrete version of colormap is just like the other versions which is helpful in a way any other colormap will be.

MULTIPLE SUBSLOTS

Multiple perspectives of data can be sighted together at the same time. So, here is the concept of subplots. Subplot consists of smaller axes that are contained in a single figure. These subplots can be something like an extensive layout of values. In this section, four routines for creating subplots in Matplotlib will be discovered.

SUBPLOTS BY HANDS

Creating axes can be built with the simple method of plt.axes. Moreover, plt.axes has an optional argument which consists of a list of four numbers in the figure synchronizing system. This number list represents left, right, bottom, width and height in the synchronizing system.

plt.subplot: Simple Grids of Subplots

To get columns and rows in a specific sequence is the dire need of almost everyone, so Matplotlib has worked out a convenient way for this. From these functions, the one on the lowest level is the *plt.subplot( ),* which creates only a single subplot within the grid. It requires three integer arguments, that is; the number of rows, the number of columns, and the index of the plot which is to be designed in this procedure.

```
for i in range(1, 7):
    plt.subplot(2, 3, i)
    plt.text(0.5, 0.5, str((2, 3, i)),
        fontsize=18, ha='center')
```

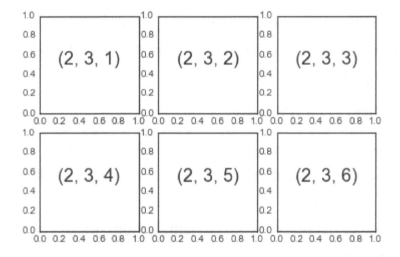

For regulating the spacing between these plots we need *plt.subplots_adjust*. For instance, hspace and wspace arguments of *plt.subplots_adjust* are used, to adjust height and width of the figure.

plt.subplots: The Whole Grid in One Go

The problem is sighted when we begin dealing with a large grid of subplots, particularly when we want to conceal x- and y-axes on the inner plot. So, *plt.subplots( )* is the one we use here for our convenience. Moreover, creating a single plot is tedious work, so the idea of creating full grids of subplots in the single line through this function is more appropriate. Arguments are the number of rows and columns which includes some additional keywords sharex and sharey, which is required to state the association of the axes.

Remember when we are specifying sharex and sharey, the inner labels are spontaneously separated from the grid to make our plot upright. So, the grid which we get as a result is within the NumPy array, which is helpful in differentiating the preferred axes using standard array indexing notation.

Comparing both subplots functions will show us that plt.subplots( ) is more compatible with Python's conventional 0-based indexing.

plt.GridSpec: More Complicated Arrangements

The plt.Gridspec( ) is the finest tool to use when taking a step ahead of the regular grids. This function works in a way that it does not generate the plot itself, it's an opportune interface that is acknowledged by the plt.subplot( ) command.

For instance, a gridspec for a grid of two rows and three columns with some defined width and height space is represented in this way.

In [8]:
grid = plt.GridSpec(2, 3, wspace=0.4, hspace=0.3)

From this location, the extent of the subplots can be set out using familiar Python slicing syntax.

TEXT AND ANNOTATION

If you have a good visualization, you can guide the reader so that the figure tells a story. Often, the story can be told in a complete visual style, without any requirement of putting an added text. However, in some cases, textual cues and labels are important. The most common yet basic types of annotations that you may include are axes labels and titles.

TRANSFORMS AND TEXT POSITION

It is mostly desirable to anchor the text to a position on the figure or axes which is independent of the data. Modification of transform is performed in Matplotlib.

There is always a scheme needed in any graphics display framework for the translation of coordination systems. These coordinate transformations are comparatively straightforward then

Any graphics display framework needs some scheme for translating between coordinate systems. For example, a data point at (x,y)=(1,1) needs to somehow be represented at a certain location on the figure, which in turn needs to be represented in pixels on the screen. Mathematically, such coordinate transformations are relatively straightforward, and Matplotlib has a well-developed set of tools that it uses internally to perform them (these tools can be explored in the matplotlib.transforms submodule).

The average user rarely needs to worry about the details of these transforms, but it is helpful knowledge to have when considering the placement of text on a figure. There are three predefined transforms that can be useful in this situation:

ax.transData: Transform associated with data coordinates

ax.transAxes: Transform associated with the axes (in units of axes dimensions)

fig.transFigure: It deals with the figure transformation.(in units of figure transformation)

By default, the text is aligned in a sequence, above and left of the particular coordinates. Notice that if axes limits are modified, the only affected coordinates will be transData coordinates, while the other remains unaffected.

This is further explained when axes limits are affected interactively. If you are going to implement that code into a notebook, its execution is done by changing *%matplotlib inline* to *%matplotlib notebook* and each plot's menu collaborate with the plot.

ARROWS AND ANNOTATIONS

Another significant annotation is a simple arrow.

Drawing arrows through matplotlib is a complicated thing to deal with. Using plt.arrow( ) to draw an arrow is intensive work. I would suggest that using plt.annotation( ) is much more suitable for performing this function, as it is more flexible in performing its function.

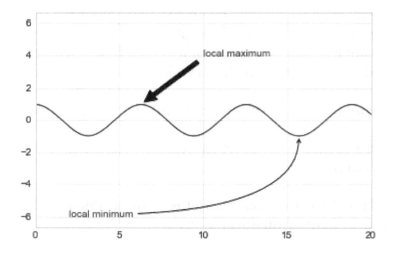

The arrow style is bound through the arrowprops dictionary, which has various options available. These options are well documented in online documentation of Matplotlib. In these documentations, the specifications of arrows and textbones are well elaborated, which ultimately results into an arrow style of your desire. Regrettably, it also requires manual modifications of its features, which can lead to a time-consuming process when producing publication-quality graphics. Concludingly, the prior mix of styles is not to be preferred for presenting data.

CUSTOMIZING TICKS

Matplotlib's formatting and ticks are not appropriate to use on many occasions. It is better to understand the Matplotlib hierarchy of objects in a plot. Matplotlib aims to have a Python object to represent everything on the plot. It also aims at having an object which performs as a single container to withhold the sub-objects. Axis have two attributes, x axis and y axis, which then in turn have attributes which contain properties like lines, labels, and ticks.

MAJOR AND MINOR TICKS

Major and a minor tick mark is another important concept within each axis. As the names imply, major ticks are more visible and prominent, while the minor ones are smaller, and less pronounced. In Matplotlib, there are more major ticks by default but there are minor ticks used within logarithm plots.

The most often used tick/label formatting operation is hiding ticks or labels. This operation is performed through plt.NullLocator() and plt.NullFormatter().

CUSTOMIZING MATPLOTLIB: CONFIGURATIONS AND STYLESHEETS

Users mostly complain about the default plot settings of Matplotlib. Though there were some changes made in the 2.0 Matplotlib release in late 2016, the capacity to customize default settings helps bring the package inline with every individual's aesthetic preferences.

CHANGING THE DEFAULTS: *rcParams*

Matplotlib defines a runtime configuration (rc) which includes the default styles for each plot element you make, every time you load Matplotlib. The configuration can be maintained using plt.rc convenience routine.

STYLESHEETS

In August 2014, the version 1.4 release of Matplotlib included a highly fitting style module which also contains a variety of new default stylesheets and the ability to make and design your own styles. The stylesheet formatting is very similar to *matplotlibrc* files; the only difference is that the file must be named with the extension. *mplstyle.*

The default included stylesheets are also highly useful even if you decide not to create your own style. Let us look at five available styles.

In [8]:
plt.style.available[:5]

Out[8]:
['fivethirtyeight',
 'seaborn-pastel',
 'seaborn-whitegrid',
 'ggplot',
 'grayscale']

FiveThirtyEightStyle AND ggplot

The fivethirtyeightstyle follows the same graphics which are found on the famous FiveThirtyEightwebsite. For example:

In [12]:
```
with plt.style.context('fivethirtyeight'):
    hist_and_lines()
```

ggplot

The ggplot package is a famous package used as a visualization tool in R language. For example:

In [13]:
```
with plt.style.context('ggplot'):
    hist_and_lines()
```

THREE DIMENSION PLOTTING IN MATPLOTLIB

Originally, Matplotlib only had a two-dimensional plotting system. It was the time when 1.0 was released that a few three-dimensional plotting utilities were constructed on top of two-dimensional display of Matplotlib and the outcome was a suitable yet limited set of tools for the visualization of three-dimensional data. The enabling of three-dimensional plots is performed through transporting the mplot3d kit, together with the main Matplotlib installation:

In [1]:
```python
from mpl_toolkits import mplot3d
```
After the submodule is taken, you can then create a three-dimensional axis by passing the keyword *projection= '3d'* to any normal axis's creation routines. For example:

In [2]:
```python
%matplotlib inline
import numpy as np
import matplotlib.pyplot as plt
```

In [3]:
```python
fig = plt.figure()
ax = plt.axes(projection='3d')
```

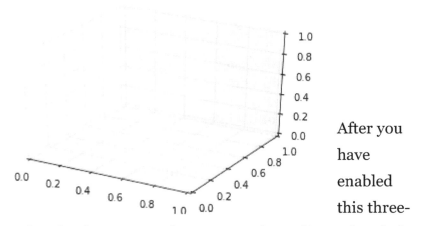

After you have enabled this three-dimensional axis, you can plot as many three-dimensional plot types. The 3d plotting is one of the developments which is aided heavily by interactively seeing figures instead of viewing it statically in the notebook.

THREE-DIMENSIONAL PLOTS AND LINES

Line or a collection of scatter plots designed from a set of (X, Y, Z) triples is considered the most basic three-dimensional plot. Such a plot can be built using *ax.plot3D* and *ax.scatter3D* functions. You may notice that the call signature for these plots is quite similar to their two-dimensional counterparts, so you can recall Simple Line Plots and Simple Scatter Plots. Let us now plot a trigonometric spiral, together with a few points drawn arbitrarily near the line:

In [4]:
```
ax = plt.axes(projection='3d')

# Data for a three-dimensional line
zline = np.linspace(0, 15, 1000)
xline = np.sin(zline)
yline = np.cos(zline)
ax.plot3D(xline, yline, zline, 'gray')

# Data for three-dimensional scattered points
zdata = 15 * np.random.random(100)
xdata = np.sin(zdata) + 0.1 * np.random.randn(100)
ydata = np.cos(zdata) + 0.1 * np.random.randn(100)
ax.scatter3D(xdata, ydata, zdata, c=zdata, cmap='Greens');
```

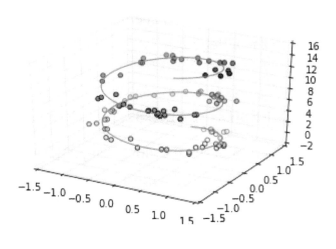

In the above example, you might notice that in default settings, scatter points have transparency attuned in such a fashion that it gives a sense of depth on the page. The three-dimensional effect is quite a times hard to view within a static image, but the interactive view can result in good intuitions about the points' layout.

GEOGRAPHIC DATA WITH BASEMAP

Geographic data visualization is a famous type of visualization in the field of data science. Basemap toolkit is the key resource for Geographic data visualization, which also, like many other Matplotlib kits, thrives under the label of *mpl_toolkits*. You might feel strange while working with Basemap because it generally takes too much time to render, but modern way outs such as leaflet or Google Maps API can prove to be an optimal choice for intensive map visualizations. Nevertheless, Basemap is still a handy tool for most of the Python users.

Basemap installation is an easy task. If you are using conda, you can download the package by typing:

```
$ conda install basemap
```

Only an addition of a single new import is required to the standard formula.

```
In [1]:
%matplotlib inline
import numpy as np
```

```
import matplotlib.pyplot as plt
from mpl_toolkits.basemap import Basemap
```

Now, when you are done with installation and import of Basemap toolkit, geographic plots are not far away. Note that the graphics in the given example requires PIL package in Python 2, and PILLOW package in Python 3:

```
In [2]:
plt.figure(figsize=(8, 8))
m = Basemap(projection='ortho', resolution=None,
lat_0=50, lon_0=-100)
m.bluemarble(scale=0.5);
```

The globe you see above is not only an image, rather it is a well-functioning Matplotlib axis that comprehends spherical coordinates and which permits the users to smoothly overplot data on the map. For example:

```
In [3]:
fig = plt.figure(figsize=(8, 8))
m = Basemap(projection='lcc', resolution=None,
        width=8E6, height=8E6,
        lat_0=45, lon_0=-100,)
m.etopo(scale=0.5, alpha=0.5)

# Map (long, lat) to (x, y) for plotting
x, y = m(-122.3, 47.6)
plt.plot(x, y, 'ok', markersize=5)
plt.text(x, y, ' Seattle', fontsize=12);
```

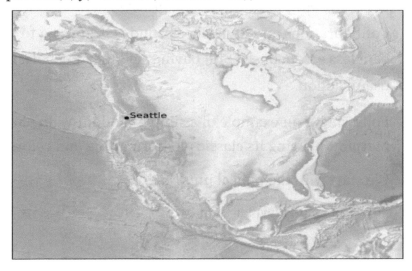

So, now you see how with a few lines of Python, a geographic visualization becomes possible.

VISUALIZATION WITH SEABORN

Seaborn came as a solution to various complaints lodged against Matplotlib such as its default choices not keeping up to the expectations, Matplotlib's API being relatively low, and its inability to visualize data from a Pandas DataFrame easily. Seaborn gives an API on the top of Matplotlib that provides its users genuine choices for plot style and color defaults. Moreover, it describes simple yet high-level functions for commonly used statistical plot types. Also, it merges with the functionality given by Pandas DataFrames.

Recently, Matplotlib added the plt.style tools such as Configurations and Style Sheets, and is beginning to handle data less erroneously. Still having said that, Seaborn is a highly useful addon.

Following is an example of a simple random-walk plot in Matplotlib, using its classic plot formatting and colors.

We start with the typical imports:

```
import matplotlib.pyplot as plt
plt.style.use('classic')
%matplotlib inline
import numpy as np
import pandas as pd
```

Now we create some random walk data:

```
# Create some data
```

```
rng = np.random.RandomState(0)
```

```
x = np.linspace(0, 10, 500)
```

```
y = np.cumsum(rng.randn(500, 6), 0)
```

And do a simple plot:

```
# Plot the data with Matplotlib defaults
```

```
plt.plot(x, y)
```

```
plt.legend('ABCDEF', ncol=2, loc='upper left');
```

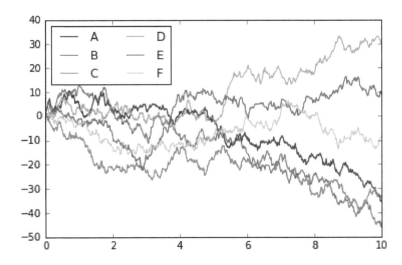

Although the result contains all the information we'd like it to convey, it does so in a way that is not all that aesthetically pleasing, and even looks a bit old-fashioned in the context of 21st-century data visualization.

Now let's take a look at how it works with Seaborn. As we will see, Seaborn has many of its own high-level plotting routines, but it can also overwrite Matplotlib's default parameters and in turn get even simple Matplotlib scripts to produce vastly superior output. We can set the style by calling Seaborn's set() method. By convention, Seaborn is imported as sns:

```
import seaborn as sns

sns.set()
```

Now let's rerun the same two lines as before:

```
# same plotting code as above!

plt.plot(x, y)

plt.legend('ABCDEF', ncol=2, loc='upper left');
```

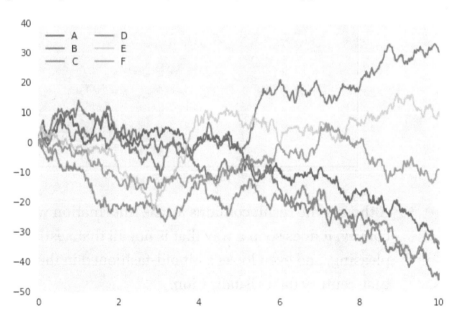

CHAPTER 5

INTRODUCTION TO DATA CLEANING AND MANIPULATIONS WITH PANDAS

MANIPULATION WITH PANDAS

Pandas is an innovation built on top of NumPy. It gives a perfect implementation of a DataFrame as well. To revise, DataFrames are multidimensional arrays with connected row and column labels, and most of the time with heterogeneous types and/or missing information. Other than providing a suitable storage interface for labeled data, Pandas also executes various powerful data operations similar to spreadsheet programs and database framework's users.

INSTALLATION AND USAGE OF PANDAS

For installing Pandas on your system, installation of NumPy is required. Combination of C and Cython sources through the suitable tools is of need when a library is to be established from source. Further information on installation is given on the *Pandas documentation*. If you are acting according to the advice outlined in the *Preface* and working with the Anaconda stack, you have installed the Pandas already.

The instant Pandas is installed you can check the version by importing it.

In [1]:
```python
import pandas
pandas.__version__
```
Out[1]:
```
'0.18.1'
```

In [2]:
```python
import pandas as pd
```

REMINDER ABOUT BUILT-IN DOCUMENTATION

The service of referring to the content of the package and the documentation of different types of functions, with greater ease is the significance of IPython. For more details on this you can refer back to Help and Documentation in Python.

INTRODUCING PANDAS OBJECTS

To understand in simplest terms, Pandas objects is an improved version of NumPy structured arrays. In it, rows and columns are defined with labels instead of simple integer indices. Also, Pandas gives its users various tools and methods on top of basic data structures. Now, let us look at a brief introduction to Series, Data Frame, and Index.

1. PANDAS SERIES OBJECTS

A Pandas Series can be taken as a one-dimensional array of indexed data. If you wish to create it from a list or arrays, this is how you do it:

```
In [2]:
data = pd.Series([0.25, 0.5, 0.75, 1.0])
data
```
Out[2]:
```
0    0.25
1    0.50
2    0.75
3    1.00
dtype: float64
```
You should notice that in the output, the *Series* contains both a sequence of values and sequence of indices. These sequences can then be accessed through *value* and *index* attributes. The *values* are same as the known NumPy array:

```
In [3]:
data.values
```
Out[3]:
```
array([ 0.25, 0.5 , 0.75, 1. ])
```

```
In [4]:
data.index
```
Out[4]:
```
RangeIndex(start=0, stop=4, step=1)
```

Data in Panda series, like with a NumPy array, can be accessed through the linked index via the same Python square-bracket notation.

In [5]:
data[1]
Out[5]:
0.5

In [6]:
data[1:3]
Out[6]:
1   0.50
2   0.75
dtype: float64

The Pandas *Series*, although copies one dimensional NumPy array, is much more flexible and easier to handle.

2. PANDAS DATAFRAME OBJECTS

Pandas DataFrame objects can also be taken as either a generalization of NumPy arrays or as a specialization of a Python dictionary.

DataFrame as generalization of NumPy array:

As we have studied earlier, Series is an analog of a one-dimensional array having comparatively flexible indices. DataFrame, on the other hand, is an analog of a two-dimensional array with not just flexible row indices, but also many flexible column indices. Therefore, you can take

DataFrame as a sequence of aligned Series objects (by aligned it means they share a similar index).

DataFrame as specialization of Python dictionary:

You are well aware that a dictionary maps a key to a certain value, but you might not know that a DataFrame maps a name of a column to a Series of column data. Also, it is wiser to take DataFrames as generalized dictionaries instead of generalized arrays.

Examples:

Constructing DataFrame from a dictionary.

```
d = {'col1': [1, 2], 'col2': [3, 4]}

df = pd.DataFrame(data=d)

df
```

```
  col1  col2

0   1    3

1   2    4
```

Notice that the inferred dtype is int64.

```
df.dtypes

col1    int64

col2    int64
```

dtype: object

To enforce a single dtype:

df = pd.DataFrame(data=d, dtype=np.int8)

df.dtypes

col1   int8

col2   int8

dtype: object

Constructing DataFrame from a dictionary including Series:

d = {'col1': [0, 1, 2, 3], 'col2': pd.Series([2, 3], index=[2, 3])}

pd.DataFrame(data=d, index=[0, 1, 2, 3])

    col1 col2

0   0 NaN

1   1 NaN

2   2 2.0

3   3 3.0

Constructing DataFrame from numpy ndarray:

df2 = pd.DataFrame(np.array([[1, 2, 3], [4, 5, 6], [7, 8, 9]]),

            columns=['a', 'b', 'c'])

df2

```
   a  b  c

0  1  2  3

1  4  5  6

2  7  8  9
```

Constructing DataFrame from a numpy ndarray that has labeled columns:

```
data = np.array([(1, 2, 3), (4, 5, 6), (7, 8, 9)],
        dtype=[("a", "i4"), ("b", "i4"), ("c", "i4")])

df3 = pd.DataFrame(data, columns=['c', 'a'])
```

```
df3

   c  a

0  3  1

1  6  4

2  9  z
```

Constructing DataFrame from dataclass:

```
from dataclasses import make_dataclass

Point = make_dataclass("Point", [("x", int), ("y", int)])

pd.DataFrame([Point(0, 0), Point(0, 3), Point(2, 3)])
```

```
   x  y
```

```
0 0 0

1 0 3

2 2 3
```

3. THE PANDAS INDEX OBJECT

Previously, you have seen how both the Series and DataFrame objects provide a detailed index which allows you to reference and enhance data. Index object has a very fascinating structure and can be understood either as an immutable array or as an ordered/multi-set. From a list of integers, let us create a construct.

```
In [30]:
ind = pd.Index([2, 3, 5, 7, 11])
ind
```

Int64Index([2, 3, 5, 7, 11], dtype='int64')

Index as immutable array

You will be surprised to know that Index, in multiple ways, functions similar to an array. For example, if you want to retrieve values or slices, you may use standard Python indexing notation:

```
In [31]:
ind[1]
Out[31]:
3
```

In [32]:
ind[::2]

Int64Index([2, 5, 11], dtype='int64')

Moreover, Index objects have several similar attributes as that of NumPy arrays:

In [33]:
print(ind.size, ind.shape, ind.ndim, ind.dtype)
5 (5,) 1 int64

The key difference between Index objects and NumPy arrays is that indices in Index are immutable, which means they cannot be enhanced through normal means:

In [34]:
ind[1] = 0

TypeError   Traceback (most recent call last)
<ipython-input-34-40e631c82e8a> in <module>()
----> 1 ind[1] = 0

/Users/jakevdp/anaconda/lib/python3.5/site-packages/pandas/indexes/base.py in __setitem__(self, key, value)
   1243
   1244   def __setitem__(self, key, value):
-> 1245   raise TypeError("Index does not support mutable operations")
   1246
   1247   def __getitem__(self, key):

`TypeError`: Index does not support mutable operations
The immutable feature of Index object makes it more convenient and reliable to share indices between more than one DataFrames and arrays, without incurring any side effects from unintentional index change.

Index as ordered set

Pandas objects are manufactured in such a style that it aids operations like joins across datasets, which are dependent on several factors of set arithmetic. The *Index* object takes after many of the typical conventions offered by Python's default data structure, so that differences, intersections, unions and several other combinations can be figured in a familiar way:

```
In [35]:
indA = pd.Index([1, 3, 5, 7, 9])
indB = pd.Index([2, 3, 5, 7, 11])
```

```
In [36]:
indA & indB  # intersection
Out[36]:
Int64Index([3, 5, 7], dtype='int64')
```

```
In [37]:
indA | indB  # union
Out[37]:
Int64Index([1, 2, 3, 5, 7, 9, 11], dtype='int64')
```

```
In [38]:
indA ^ indB  # symmetric difference
```

Int64Index([1, 2, 9, 11], dtype='int64')

The operations above can also be retrieved by object methods, for example *indA.intersection(indB)*.

DATA INDEXING AND SELECTION

We will be viewing some methods to access and modify the values in Pandas Series and Dataframes. Firstly, we will look at one-dimensional Series objects. Secondly, we will be working with a two-dimensional Dataframe object.

DATA SELECTION IN SERIES

In the previous section, we have learned Series object methods. Now, keeping those methods in mind, we can work out the analogy to understand the patterns of data indexing and selection in arrays.

SERIES AS DICTIONARY

We can access dictionary-like Python expressions and methods to analyze the keys. Moreover, Series objects can be altered as a dictionary-like syntax. Its modifying features assist us to work with convenience.

SERIES AS ONE-DIMENSIONAL ARRAY

Series is built on the dictionary-like interface, to provide us with the array-style item through the basic mechanisms of NumPy arrays. For instance, *slicing by explicit indexing*:

```
# slicing by explicit index
data['a':'c']
Out[7]:
a    0.25
b    0.50
c    0.75
dtype: float64
In [8]:
```

This explicit indexing can root for confusions in the output we are getting as a result.

INDEXERS: LOC, ILOC, AND IX

These slicing and indexing conventions can be a cause of confusion in most cases. Pandas is successful in finding out the suitable solution to this problem by introducing us with special *indexer* attributes. The first one is, *loc* attribute, which helps in indexing and slicing that always references the explicit index:

```
data.loc[1]
Out[14]:
'a'

In [15]:
data.loc[1:3]
Out[15]:
```

```
1   a
3   b
dtype: object
```
Similarly, iloc attributes assist in slicing and indexing that always references the implicit Python-style index.

One thing to remember here is that explicit is better than implicit as it helps us in maintaining clean and readable code.

DATA SELECTION IN DATAFRAME

DataFrames can work out with two-dimensional arrays and also as a dictionary of Series structures sharing the same index.

DATAFRAME AS A DICTIONARY

The columns of DataFrame are formed through individual series which are retrieved through the dictionary-style indexing of the column name. Similarly, attributes-style column names can also be accessed. However, it is not reliable in all cases.

Specifically, you should suppress the urge to try column assignment through attributes.

DATAFRAME AS A TWO-DIMENSIONAL ARRAY

As we know, DataFrame can deal with two-dimensional arrays.

When indexing of DataFrame objects is to be done, the dictionary-style indexing of columns prevents us from dealing with it as a simple NumPy array. Specifically, passing a single index to an array accesses a row:

```
 data.values[0]
Out[26]:
array([  4.23967000e+05,   3.83325210e+07,
9.04139261e+01])
```

Thus, for array-style indexing, Pandas take advantage of loc, iloc and ix indexers. The ix indexer is the hybrid of previous two approaches.

Notice that ix indexer faces the similar potential sources of ambiguity as discussed for integer-indexed Series object.

Working smoothly with Pandas data manipulation, my suggestion is to spend more time with simple Dataframe and seeking types of indexing, slicing and masking.

ADDITIONAL INDEXING CONVENTIONS

There are many more indexing methods which may not seem in harmony to the previous methods, but are of significance in most cases.

As slices refers to rows, this can be done by numbers rather than by index:

data[1:3]

	area	pop	density
Florida	170312	19552860	114.806121
Illinois	149995	12882135	85.883763

Likewise, direct masking operations are also depicted row-wise rather than column-wise.

data[data.density > 100]
Out[35]:

	area	pop	density
Florida	170312	19552860	114.806121
New York	1412 97	19651127	139.076746

These two conventions are of importance, although they may not match the Pandas conventions, but are quite useful.

OPERATING ON DATA IN PANDAS

Pandas inherit much of the functions of NumPy and the Ufuncs. However, for *unary functions* and *binary functions,* Ufuncs will *preserve index* and *align indices.*

UFUNCS: INDEX PRESERVATION

As Pandas is known to work on the same design as NumPy, so any NumPy ufunc will deal with Pandas Dataframe and Series objects. Applying a NumPy ufunc on either of these two objects, you will get another Panda object with *indices preserved.*

np.exp(ser)

Out[4]:

```
0    403.428793
1     20.085537
2   1096.633158
3     54.598150
dtype: float64
```

Moreover, other Ufuncs discussed in previous sections, can also be of significance here.

UFUNCS: INDEX ALIGNMENT

As discussed before, Pandas align indices when dealing with binary operations. To have a better understanding about Pandas binary operations, you can refer to its examples.

Ufuncs: Operations Between DataFrame and Series

When working between these two objects, Pandas maintain index and column alignment in the same manner. These types of operations are similar to the operations held between one-dimensional and two-dimensional NumPy arrays.

Consider a simple operation of finding the difference of a two-dimensional array and one of its rows. According to NumPy broadcasting rules, this subtraction is applied row-wise.

If you are considering applying it column-wise rather than row-wise, you can use objects methods discussed before. For this you have to specify the axis keyword:

df.subtract(df['R'], axis=0)

	Q	R	S	T
0	-5	0	-6	-4
1	-4	0	-2	2
2	5	0	2	7

Concludingly, we infer that Pandas will always maintain data context in its operations to avoid some common type of errors.

HANDLING MISSING DATA

Here we will be discussing some common considerations for missing data and how different sources represent this missing data in different ways. Adding to it, some built-in tools of Pandas will also be discussed here which are responsible for handling missing data in Python.

TRADE-OFFS IN MISSING DATA CONVENTIONS

There are two commonly known schemes for indicating this missing data. These two approaches are *masking approach* and *sentinel approach*.

Masking approach refers to the allocation of one bit in the data representation to specify null status of the value.

Whereas, *Sentinel approach* refers to indication of a missing integer value through some odd bit pattern, or specifying through NaN, a special value which is part of IEEE floating-point specification.

None of these schemes are without the trade-offs. Masking scheme demands an additional Boolean array, while the sentinel scheme deducts the range of valid values that can be displayed and can also demand extra logic in CPU and GPU arithmetic.

MISSING DATA IN PANDAS

Pandas' way of handling the missing data can be restricted because of its dependency on the NumPy package.

Pandas can follow R's lead, but it is a difficult approach as it demands specification of bit patterns for each of the data types to indicate nullness. However, NumPy can deal with a number of basic integer types than the R's lead which could only handle four basic types of integers at once. Still, NumPy's approach is ungainly due to its cumbersome amount of overhead in special-casing a variety of operations for various types.

NumPy can deal with masked arrays, but the overhead in both storage, computation, and code maintenance makes it an unreliable approach.

With keeping all these restrictions in view, Pandas go for sentinels for missing data. Adding to it, it further opts for two already-existing Python null values: the special floating-point *NaN* value, and the Python *None* object.

None: Pythonic missing data

The foremost sentinel used by Pandas is *None*. As we know, *None* is a Python object, so it can only be used in arrays with data type *object*.

```
import numpy as np
import pandas as pd
```

In [2]:
vals1 = np.array([1, **None**, 3, 4])
vals1

Out[2]:
array([1, None, 3, 4], dtype=object)

The dtype=object means that the most common type of representation NumPy could deduce for the contents of the array is they are Python objects.

Python objects in an array are quite useful in performing aggregations.

NaN: Missing numerical data

The other missing data representation is dealt through the special floating-point value that works with standard IEEE floating-point representation.

You will see that NumPy opts for native floating-point type for this array as this array supports swift operations pushed into compiled code.

NaN AND NONE IN PANDAS

Nan and None perform in Pandas interchangeably, where they perform as required.

For such types which don't have sentinel values available, Pandas had to manually typecast the NA values present.

Pandas casting approach performs really well without causing issues.

OPERATING ON NULL VALUES

As we have seen that Nan and None values can be used interchangeably, so to add to its significance, there are some useful methods of removing, detecting and replacing null values in Pandas data structures.

DETECTING NULL VALUES

For detection of null data, there are two useful methods in Pandas: isnull() and notnull( ). These two methods will produce similar Boolean results for the Dataframe index.

DROPPING NULL VALUES

There are two other methods, dropna() and fillna(). The dropna() method makes available to you a number of options in Dataframe, rather than restricting yourself to a particular option.

There is a threshold parameter for specifying a minimum number of non-null values for the rows/column to be kept.

FILLING NULL VALUES

On some occasions, it is better to fill null values, rather than dropping them out. Filling out can also be done by a simple zero. This is worked out through the isnull() method as a mask, but it is very common, we can switch to fillna() method.

HIERARCHICAL INDEXING

As we have learned previously how to handle one-dimensional and two-dimensional data, it is useful to master how we should tackle multiple-dimensional data. Hierarchical indexing is one of the useful methods which is helpful in tackling multi-dimensional data.

THE BETTER WAY: PANDAS MULTIINDEX

Luckily, Pandas provide a better way for multi-indexing. Pandas offer a number of operations we desire for. Let us see how to create a MultiIndex from tuples:

```
In [5]:
index = pd.MultiIndex.from_tuples(index)
index
Out[5]:
MultiIndex(levels=[['California', 'New York', 'Texas'], [2000,
2010]],
        labels=[[0, 0, 1, 1, 2, 2], [0, 1, 0, 1, 0, 1]])
```

Have you noticed the multiple levels of indexing in the MultiIndex? In the above example, the levels are the names of state and years, and also the multiple labels which perform the encoding.

You can see a hierarchical representation of the data once you re-index your series with this MultiIndex:

In [6]:
pop = pop.reindex(index)
pop
Out[6]:
California 2000   33871648
           2010   37253956
New York   2000   18976457
           2010   19378102
Texas   2000   20851820
           2010   25145561
dtype: int64

In the above case, the first two columns of the *Series* representation depict the various index values, whereas the third column represents the data. There are a few entries missing in the first column because in such a multi-index representation, any such blank entries have the similar value as the line above it.

COMBINING DATASETS

Combining different data sources can give some amazing results. Combination may be of two different datasets or intricate database-style joins. This kind of operation is strictly kept in mind when dealing with the creation of Series and DataFrames. Moreover, Pandas have certain built-in methods and functions that can make this type of data concatenation simple and quick. Let us now look at a very basic example of wrangling of *Series* and *DataFrames* with the *pd.concat* function. We will make use of standard imports below:

In [1]:
```
import pandas as pd
import numpy as np
```

In [2]:
```
def make_df(cols, ind):
    """Quickly make a DataFrame"""
    data = {c: [str(c) + str(i) for i in ind]
            for c in cols}
    return pd.DataFrame(data, ind)

# example DataFrame
make_df('ABC', range(3))
```
Out[2]:

	A	B	C
0	A0	B0	C0
1	A1	B1	C1
2	A2	B2	C2

SIMPLE CONCATENATION WITH *PD.CONCAT*

Pd.concat() is another major function of Pandas which has an identical syntax to *np.concatenate*. However, it comprises of variable options that we will mention below:

```
# Signature in Pandas v0.18

pd.concat(objs, axis=0, join='outer', join_axes=None,
ignore_index=False,

    keys=None, levels=None, names=None,
verify_integrity=False,

    copy=True)
```

Pd.concat() is often used for combining Series or DataFrame objects, just as np.concatenate() is used for simple combination of arrays:

```
In [6]:
ser1 = pd.Series(['A', 'B', 'C'], index=[1, 2, 3])
ser2 = pd.Series(['D', 'E', 'F'], index=[4, 5, 6])
pd.concat([ser1, ser2])
Out[6]:
1   A
2   B
3   C
4   D
5   E
6   F
```

dtype: object
The same function also works for concatenating higher-dimensional objects, like DataFrames:

```
In [7]:
df1 = make_df('AB', [1, 2])
df2 = make_df('AB', [3, 4])
display('df1', 'df2', 'pd.concat([df1, df2])')
```

Out[7]:

df1

	A	B
1	A1	B1
2	A2	B2

df2

	A	B
3	A3	B3
4	A4	B4

pd.concat([df1, df2])

	A	B
1	A1	B1
2	A2	B2
3	A3	B3

	A	B
4	A4	B4

The process of concatenation is performed row-wise within the DataFrame (i.e., axis=0). Pd.concat also permits specification of an axis along which concatenation is to take place. For example:

In [8]:
df3 = make_df('AB', [0, 1])
df4 = make_df('CD', [0, 1])
display('df3', 'df4', "pd.concat([df3, df4], axis='col')")

Out[8]:
df3

	A	B
0	A0	B0
1	A1	B1

df4

	C	D
0	C0	D0
1	C1	D1

pd.concat([df3, df4], axis='col')

	A	B	C	D
0	A0	B0	C0	D0
1	A1	B1	C1	D1

COMBINING DATASET: MERGE AND JOIN

Another important function performed by Pandas is, memory-join and merge operations. For this purpose pd.merge is used.

CATEGORIES OF JOINS

The pd.merge function device has a number of types: the one to one, many to one, and many to many joins. All of them are retrieved through the pd.merge interface.

SPECIFICATION OF THE MERGE KEY

It finds one or more matching column names between the inputs, and apply it as a key. Unfortunately, mostly the column names are not matched. So, pd.merge offers multiple operations for this. Some of the keywords used are; on keyword, the left_on keyword, the right_on keyword, the left_index and right_index keyword.

AGGREGATION AND GROUPING

Efficient summarization holds significance in analyzation of data. So, computation aggregations are there to carry out this job.

Simple aggregation used in NumPy's array which commonly deals with one or two-dimensional structures.

However, we have Groupby functions: split, apply and combine.

Split refers to breaking and grouping a DataFrame.

Apply refers to some type of computation, usually an aggregate.

Combine refers to simply combining these operations results.

Moreover, Groupby consists of some other functions as well. Those are; filter, transform, and apply. These functions are not alike to the previous aggregations as they involve implementing multiple operations before combining the grouped data.

PIVOT TABLES

Spreadsheets and various programs that function on tabular data often use an operation called Pivot table. A pivot table uses column-wise data as its input and then groups those entries into a two-dimensional table which then gives a multidimensional summary of the data. Users may confuse pivot tables with GroupBy because these two are quite similar. If you are mixing up the two too, then you should assume that pivot tables are a multidimensional version of GroupBy aggregation. This means that you split-apply-combine, but the function of splitting and combining happens across a two-dimensional grid and not a one-dimensional index.

VECTORIZED STRING OPERATIONS

A key asset of Python is the efficient and easy process through which it handles and manipulates string data. Therefore, Pandas provides its users an encompassing set of vectorized string operations that prove to be an important piece of the kind of munging needed when dealing with real-world data.

PANDAS STRING OPERATIONS

Vectorization of operations in Pandas simplifies the syntax of working on data arrays. This means we are no longer required to be concerned about the size or shape of the array. Instead, just focus on what operation you want to execute.

Pandas, unlike NumPy, introduces us to features that fulfill the requirement for vectorized string operations and also are optimal for accurately handling data via the *str* attribute of Pandas Series and string containing Index objects. Now let us look at an example:

In [4]:
import pandas as pd
names = pd.Series(data)
names

Out[4]:
0   peter
1   Paul
2   None
3   MARY
4   gUIDO
dtype: object

There is a single method that can capitalize all the above entries:

In [5]:
names.str.capitalize()

Out[5]:
0   Peter
1   Paul
2   None
3   Mary
4   Guido
dtype: object

On the *str* attribute, if you use tab completion, it will give you a list of all the vectorized string methods available on Pandas.

HIGH PERFORMANCE PANDAS: EVAL() AND QUERY()

In January 2014, version 0.13 of Pandas was released which contained some experimental tools that permit you to directly operate on C-speed operations with cheap allocation of intermediate arrays. These functions go by the name eval() and query(); these functions depend upon the Numexpr package.

The eval() function makes use of string expressions to effectively compute operations using DataFrames. Query() function provides a more efficient computation because of its greater ease in comprehensibility. The query() function can also take in @ flag to mark local variables.

CHAPTER 6

SQL AND DATABASE QUESTIONS AND PREP

INTRODUCTION TO SQL AND DATABASES:

SQL (Structured Query Language) is a standard language that is used for retrieving and manipulating the databases. In 1986, SQL became the standard for American National Institute (ANSI), and in 1987, it was officially marked as standard by the International Organization for Standardization.

Talking about its function, SQL can carry out many functions:

1. It can carry out queries against a database
2. It can extract data from a database
3. It can insert, update and delete records from a database
4. It can make a new database.
5. SQL can make new tables in a database
6. SQL can create stored procedures in a database
7. SQL can create views in a database
8. SQL can set permissions on tables, procedures, and views

BIG COMPANIES THAT USE SQL

Companies for which SQL plays a crucial role includes: *Microsoft, NTT Data, Cognizant, Dell, Accenture, and Stack overflow*.

SQL USED BY COMPANIES

These companies do not write SQL for their databases, rather they choose a database system which consists of built-in SQL. *MySQL*, facilitates these companies by providing them with a developed database system as it is one of the most popular one currently available.

SIGNIFICANCE OF SQL TO MARKETERS

Marketers use SQL to group users based on their characteristics and to deduce perception regarding them. IN other words, it is majorly used for segmentation by marketers.

WHY SQL ISN'T GOING ANYWHERE

The reason why SQL isn't going anywhere is due to its practical approach. It brings us an exceptional choice of options to perform. Moreover, there is no viable substitute available at hand to replace SQL which provides absolute adaptability, complete power and pure convenience to users.

SQL's UNIVERSALITY

SQL's universality and acceptability, has proven its practicality. This points out that much thought has been given to SQL, while it was being designed. Although it has gone under some changes in this time, it has only helped users to understand and use SQL more easily.

For this reason, SQL is still out there to facilitate its users.

WHY SHOULD I LEARN SQL FOR DATA SCIENCE?

SQL fame is still in the air, we have learned that in the previous section. We are bound to learn SQL for data science as it has become a major requirement of many renowned companies. For instance, most of the companies store their data in a Relational Database Management System (RDBMS) and it demands SQL to access it.

ADOPTION OF SQL BY CURRENT TECHNOLOGY

Most importantly, SQL is embraced by newer technology, such as Hive, a SQL-like query language to query and handle the large datasets.

Moreover, SQL learning follows the "learn once, use anywhere" principle. So, SQL learning holds much significance. Adding to it, SQL is not even harder to learn, not even hard for beginners.

SQL SYNTAX: SELECT, WHERE, COMPARE statements, Logical operators, LIKE, IN operators, BETWEEN, IS NULL, AND, OR, NOT, ORDER BY

These all are a part of SQL inquiry. *SELECT* refers to an indication of the column you would like to view.

```
SELECT year,
month,
west
```

This type of syntax doesn't need to be capitalized. SQL will understand it, even when you write it in simple form.
Next step is to filter the data. To perform this function WHERE is used here. "*" mean all columns

```
SELECT *
 FROM tutorial.us_housing_units
    WHERE month = 1
```

This type of syntax is helpful in Excel, where we want to reorder the columns. It filters based on values in one column. Results in all columns will be limited to rows that fulfill the requirement.

The most common way of filtering data is to use comparison operators. Its real time significance can be viewed, when applied to numerical columns.

SELECT *
 FROM tutorial.us_housing_units
   WHERE west > 30

Logical operators are needed when you need to use a number of comparison operators in one query. To apply these logical operators in SQL, you can use data from *Billboard Music Charts*.

LIKE allows you to match on similar values rather than exact ones.

SELECT *
 FROM tutorial.billboard_top_100_year_end
   WHERE "group" LIKE 'Snoop%'

 Likewise, IN is another logical operator which assists you in specifying the values in the list you wish to add up in the result.

Then comes BETWEEN logical operators. It helps you to opt only for rows that are in a particular range. It usually works with an AND operator.

IS NULL is of significance, when rows with missing data are needed to be removed.

Any operation which equals NULL will not work, because arithmetic is not performed on null values.

AND operator refers to selecting only rows that fulfill two conditions.

SELECT *
 FROM tutorial.billboard_top_100_year_end
 WHERE year = 2012 AND year_rank <= 10

This type of logical operator is usually used by collaboration of some other comparison operator with AND operator.

OR operator that helps you indicate rows that fulfill either of the two requirements. Otherwise, it works in the same way as the AND operator.

However, NOT is a logical operator in SQL which can be situated before a conditional statement to select rows for which that particular statement is false. NOT is usually operated with LIKE.

After understanding filtration of data, it is necessary to learn how to reorder your data. The ORDER BY logical operator helps you sort out the results based on the data in one or more columns.

```
SELECT *
 FROM tutorial.billboard_top_100_year_end
 ORDER BY artist
```

This type of operator works in ascending order which is by default.

GIVE EXAMPLES OF EACH SQL CLAUSE AND OPERATORS

COMMON DATABASE OR MY SQL QUESTIONS

1. DEFINE SQL?

Answer: SQL is an abbreviation of Structured Query Language. It is a query language specially for managing data in RDBMS.

2. WHAT IS RDBMS?

Answer: It is abbreviated as Relational Database Management System. It is the most widely used system.

3. WHAT IS DATA MINING?

Answer: It performs its function by drawing out information from the data set and converting it into human readable form.

4. WHAT IS ERD?

Answer: It stands for Entity Relationship Diagram. It is basically the graphical representation of tables.

5. HOW TO STORE A PICTURE FILE IN THE DATABASE?

Answer: It is not a good idea to store pictures in the database. However, the object type 'Blob' is recommended.

6. HOW MANY TRIGGERS ARE POSSIBLE IN MYSQL?

Answer: Only six types of triggers are used in MySQL:

- Before insert
- After insert
- Before Update
- After Update
- Before Delete
- After Delete

7. WHAT IS HEAP TABLE?

Answer: Tables displayed in tables are called HEAP tables. They make use of indexes which makes it faster.

ADVANCED DATABASE QUESTIONS

1. WHY USE MYSQL DATABASE SERVER?

Answer: It is very fast and easy to use. Its software can easily be modified.

2. WHAT ARE TECHNICAL FEATURES OF MYSQL SERVER?

Answer: It is a client/server system that contains a multi-threaded SQL server that provides backup to different backends and APIs.

3. HOW DO YOU RETURN THE HUNDRED BOOKS STARTING FROM 25th?

Answer: SELECT book_title FROM books LIMIT 25, 100;

4. WHAT IS A DEFAULT PORT FOR MYSQL SERVER?

Answer: The default port is 3306.

CHAPTER 7

STATISTICS AND PROBABILITY

BASIC STATISTICS

In simple words, statistics is the study of data. Basic statistics lay the foundation for the further studies on this subject. It refers to collection of methods: collecting, displaying, analyzing and collecting data to deduce a conclusion.

WHAT IS EXPECTED FROM A DATA SCIENTIST?

A data scientist should be able to compile and analyze large data sets. He should know the technicalities of programming, machine learning, data visualization and so on. They are capable of interpreting data with the help of tools and methods from statistics.

HOW DO WE USE STATS IN OUR DAILY LIFE?

Statistics play a crucial role in our daily lives. Statistics can be used in medical studies, it is used for predicting weather forecasting, it assists in stock markets and also for consumer goods. Moreover, it has much significance in the field of politics. A news channel shows the results of the election with the assistance of statistical data.

INTRO TO PROBABILITY, BASIC PROBABILITY OF DATA SCIENCE

It is true that the journey of the study of statistics can't be initiated without probability. Probability is defined as, how likely an event is. For instance, if there is 60% chance that A team will win from B team, it means, A team has a probability of 0.6.

For calculating the likeliness of an event which is to happen, we need a proper framework to present the outcome in numbers. Random variables are mostly used for this purpose.

Just suppose X to be the outcome of a coin toss.

X = outcome of a coin toss

Possible Outcomes:

- 1 if heads
- 0 if tail

Sometimes we face the situation of pass-fail. You either win or lose the game. For instance, your cricket team plays five test matches against your opponent team. Whoever wins more games out of five, that team will win. This is called Binomial distribution.

But on some occasions, you will encounter larger sets of data which can be dealt with easily. You can opt for the little part of that data to work with but it will not be convenient. So, the Central limit theorem is of significance here.

WHY SHOULD I LEARN PROBABILITY FOR DATA SCIENCE?

Probability lays the mathematical foundation for the data analyzation in statistics. With the assistance of probability and statistics, a data scientist is capable of computing data. It is considered to be the backbone of crucial topics in data science, like inferential statistics to Bayesian networks. It helps to analyze chance events, because randomness is found everywhere.

PROBABILITY IN OUR DAILY LIVES

It is true that probability helps you in your daily life. Its significance is valued in weather forecasting, sports, online shopping, indicating blood groups, etc. Furthermore, it is valued in determining the chance of getting a job in a particular year. Even playing cards requires the use of probability.

PROBABILITY INTERVIEW QUESTIONS

1. Bobo the amoeba has a 25%, 25%, and 50% chance of producing 0, 1, or 2 offspring, respectively. Each of Bobo's descendants also have the same probabilities. What is the probability that Bobo's lineage dies out?

$p=1/4+1/4p+1/2p^\wedge2 => p=1/2$

2. In any 15-minute interval, there is a 20% probability that you will see at least one shooting star. What is the proba- bility that you see at least one shooting star in the period of an hour?

$1-(0.8)^\wedge4$. Or, we can use Poisson processes

3. How can you generate a random number between 1 - 7 with only a die?

Launch it 3 times: each throw sets the nth bit of the result.

For each launch, if the value is 1-3, record a 0, else 1. The result is between 0 (000) and 7 (111), evenly spread (3 independent throw). Repeat the throws if 0 was obtained: the process stops on evenly spread values.

4. You have a 50-50 mixture of two normal distributions with the same standard deviation. How far apart do the means need to be in order for this distribution to be bimodal?

more than two standard deviations

6. Given draws from a normal distribution with known parameters, how can you simulate draws from a uniform distribution?

plug in the value to the CDF of the same random variable

7. A certain couple tells you that they have two children, at least one of which is a girl. What is the probability that they have two girls?

1/3

8. You have a group of couples that decide to have children until they have their first girl, after which

they stop having children. What is the expected gender ratio of the children that are born? What is the expected number of children each couple will have?

The gender ratio is 1:1. Expected number of children is 2. let X be the number of children until getting a female (happens with prob 1/2). this follows a geometric distribution with probability 1/2

9. How many ways can you split 12 people into 3 teams of 4?

The outcome follows a multinomial distribution with n=12 and k=3. but the classes are indistinguishable.

STATISTICS INTERVIEW QUESTIONS

1. In an A/B test, how can you check if assignment to the various buckets was truly random?

Plot the distributions of multiple features for both A and B and make sure that they have the same shape. More rigorously, we can conduct a permutation test to see if the distributions are the same.

MANOVA to compare different means

2. What would be the hazards of letting users sneak a peek at the other bucket in an A/B test?

The user might not act the same way if they had not seen the other bucket. You are essentially adding additional variables of whether the user peeked the other bucket, which are not random across groups.

3. What would be some issues if blogs decide to cover one of your experimental groups?

Same as the previous question. The above problem can happen in larger scale.

4. How would you conduct an A/B test on an opt-in feature?

Ask for more details.

5. How would you run an A/B test for many variants, say 20 or more?

one control, 20 treatments, if the sample size for each group is big enough.

Ways to attempt to correct for this include changing your confidence level (e.g. Bonferroni Correction) or doing family-wide tests before you dive in to the individual metrics (e.g. Fisher's Protected LSD).

CHAPTER 8

PREDICTIVE MODELING AND MACHINE LEARNING QUESTIONS

Predictive modeling and machine learning are included in the most exciting fields in data science today. Predictive modeling is the process of using models to analyze historical data and make predictions about future outcomes. Machine learning is a subtype of computer science that deals with software development that can learn without being explicitly programmed.

Prediction is the ability to project the likely outcome of a future event. It is a cornerstone of the business and can be achieved in various ways. A survey of current job postings shows that data scientists are most likely to be hired to develop algorithms that can make accurate predictions based on past data. This article will explore the difference between predictive modeling and machine learning, highlight the primary areas of specialization, and outline the basic tasks.

FUNDAMENTAL STEPS IN A PREDICTIVE MODELING

Following are the steps:
1. Set the business goal of a predictive model
2. Pull Historical Data

- Internal
- External
1. Select Observation and Performance Window
2. Make new derived variables
3. Divide Data into Training, Validation, and Test Samples
4. Clean Data
5. Variable Reduction/Selection
6. Variable Transformation
7. Design Model
8. Validate Model
9. Check Model Performance
10. Deploy Model
11. Monitor Model

Moreover, predictive modeling uses in the following areas:
1. Acquisition - Cross Sell/Up Sell
2. Retention - Predictive Attrition Model
3. Customer Lifetime Value Model
4. Segment customers established on their homogenous attributes.
5. Next Best Offer
6. Underwriting
7. Campaign Response Model
8. Optimization
9. Usage Simulation
10. Market Mix Model
11. Pricing Model
12. Probability of Customers defaulting on the loan
13. Demand Forecasting

PREDICTIVE MODELING INTERVIEW QUESTIONS

1. Differentiate between Linear and Logistic Regression

There are the following differences between Linear and Logistic Regression:

1. Linear regression needs the dependent variable, likewise numeric values with no categories or groups. In comparison, Binary logistic regression needs the dependent variable to be binary - two types only (0/1). Multinomial or ordinary logistic regression has a dependent parameter with more than two categories.
2. Linear regression is founded on least square estimation, which says regression coefficients should be selected to minimize the aggregate of the squared distances of each observed response to its fitted value. However, logistic regression establishes a Maximum Likelihood Estimation. According to it, we can select coefficients in such a way that they increase the probability of Y given X (likelihood)

2. How to handle missing values?

You can handle missing values by using the following methods.

1. For Continuous Variables
   - Mean Imputation
   - Median Imputation
   - Cluster Imputation
   - Imputation with a random value
   - Impute Continuous Variables with Zero
   - Conditional Mean Imputation
2. For Categorical Variables
   - WOE for missing values
   1. Decision Tree, Random Forest, Logistic Regression
   2. Decision Tree, Random Forest works (It is for both continuous and categorical variables).

3. How to treat outliers?

There are numerous methods to treat outliers:
1. Percentile Capping
2. Box-Plot Method
3. Mean plus-minus 3 Standard Deviation
4. Weight of Evidence

4. Explain Dimensionality/Variable Reduction Methods

There are two types of dimensionality/variable methods:
1. Unsupervised Method or No Dependent Variable
2. Supervised Method or In respect to Dependent Variable

5. Explain different Unsupervised Methods
1. Principal Component Analysis (PCA)
2. Hierarchical Variable Clustering (Proc Varclus in SAS)
3. Variance Inflation Factor (VIF)
4. Remove zero and near-zero variance predictors
5. Mean absolute correlation

6. Explain Supervised Method
It divides into two categories:
1. For Binary / Categorical Dependent Variable
- Information Value
- Wald Chi-Square
- Random Forest Variable Importance
- Gradient Boosting Variable Importance
- Forward, backward or stepwise - Variable Significance
- AIC/BIC score

2. For Continuous Dependent Variable
1. Adjusted R-Square
2. Mallows' Cp Statistic
3. Random Forest Variable Importance
4. AIC / BIC score
5. Forward, backward or stepwise - variable significance

7. Define multicollinearity and how to deal with it?

Multicollinearity indicates a high correlation among independent variables. It includes the hypotheses in linear and logistic regression. It can be recognized by looking at the VIF score of variables.
- VIF > 2.5 indicates a moderate collinearity issue.
- VIF >5 is regarded as high collinearity.

8. What are the steps for calculating VIF?
Following are the steps:
1. Run linear regression is present in which one of the independent variables is known as the target variable, whereas other independent variables are independent variables.
2. Calculate variables by the following formula
   VIF = 1/(1-R-squared)

9. Do we remove intercepts during finding VIF
No, we do not remove intercepts during finding VIF. It bases on the intercept because there is an intercept in the regression, which utilizes to find VIF. When the intercept is eliminated, R-square is still worthwhile.

10. Define the p-value and its usage for variable selection.
The p-value is the lowest level of value at which you can refuse the null hypothesis. In independent variables, it implies whether the coefficient of a variable is quite diverse from zero.

11. Differentiate between Factor Analysis and PCA.
Following are the difference between Factor Analysis and PCA:

1. In Principal Components Analysis, the components are figured as linear combinations of the original variables. In Factor Analysis, the actual variables are expressed as linear combinations of the factors.
2. Principal Components Analysis is employed as a variable reduction technique; however, Factor Analysis is operated to comprehend what constructs underlie the data.
3. In Principal Components Analysis, the purpose is to explain as much of the total variance in the variables as possible. The main objective of Factor Analysis is to define the covariances or correlations among different variables.

12. Explain Fisher Scoring in Logistic Regression.

Logistic regression calculations are estimated by increasing the likelihood function. The maximization of the likelihood is achieved by an iterative process known as Fisher's scoring. It is an optimization method.

There are mainly two famous iterative processes for calculating the parameters of nonlinear equations, which are as follows -

1. Fisher's Scoring
2. Newton-Raphson

Both are similar except that Newton-Raphson employs a matrix of second-order by-products of the log-likelihood function, and Fisher operates Information Matrix. The default optimization process in PROC LOGISTIC is Fisher's Scoring in SAS.

The algorithm ends when the convergence criterion is done or when the maximum number of iterations has been reached. Convergence is acquired when the contrast between the log-likelihood function from one iteration to the next is short.

Machine Learning Interview Questions

1. Explain different types of Machine Learning?
There are three types of machine learning:
1. Supervised Learning
2. Unsupervised Learning
3. Reinforcement Learning

2. Explain all types of machine learning.
a. Supervised Learning
It is a method in which the machine learns by utilizing labeled data or learning under the guidance of a teacher.
b. Unsupervised Learning
Unsupervised learning is how the machine is trained on unlabelled data without guidance.
c.Reinforcement Learning
Reinforcement learning concerns an agent that correlates with its surroundings by creating actions and finding errors or rewards.

3. Explain the comparison between Deep Learning and Machine Learning.
Deep Learning is a kind of machine learning that is encouraged by the structure of the human brain and is especially practical in feature detection. In contrast, Machine Learning is related to algorithms that link to data, learn from it, and apply what they have understood to make informed decisions.

4. Define false negative, false positive, true negative, and confirmed positive with a simple example.
True Positive: If the alarm shifts on in case of a fire.
False Positive: If the alarm shifts on and there are no fire.

False Negative: If there is no ring on the alarm, there is a fire.

True Negative: If there is also no ring on the alarm and there is no fire.

5. Define Confusion Matrix?

A confusion matrix or an error matrix is a table used to summarize the implementation of a classification algorithm.

6. Elaborate on the comparison between inductive and deductive learning.

Inductive learning is the method of utilizing observations to conclude; however, Deductive learning is the method of operating findings to form statements.

7. Explain the difference between Gini Impurity and Entropy in a Decision Tree?

Gini Impurity and Entropy are the metrics utilized for determining how to divide a Decision Tree. Gini measurement is the possibility of a random sample being organized correctly if you randomly select a label regarding the distribution in the branch. In addition, Entropy is a parameter to calculate the absence of information. You can estimate the knowledge gained by doing a split—such measurements aid in decreasing the uncertainty about the output label.

8. Describe the contrast between Entropy and Information Gain?

Entropy is a parameter to measure how messy your data is. It lowers as you reach closer to the leaf node. However, the Information Gain is established on the reduction in Entropy after a dataset is split on an attribute.

9. What are collinearity and multicollinearity?

Collinearity happens when two predictor variables, such as x1 and x2, in multiple regression, have some correlation. In comparison, multicollinearity occurs when more than two predictor variables, likewise x1, x2, and x3, are inter-correlated.

10. Explain Eigenvectors and Eigenvalues?
Eigenvectors are vectors whose direction remains intact even when a linear transformation is conducted on them. Whereas, Eigenvalue is the scalar utilized for the change of an Eigenvector.

11. Define A/B Testing?
A/B is Statistical hypothesis testing for a randomized experiment with two parameters, A and B, which compare two models that employ various predictor variables to check which variable fits best for a given sample of data.

12. What is Cluster Sampling?
Cluster Sampling is a process of randomly choosing intact groups within a defined population, transferring comparable characteristics. For instance, when you cluster the total number of managers in a set of companies, managers will show elements, and companies will represent clusters.

13. How are NumPy and SciPy related?
NumPy describes arrays and some essential numerical functions such as indexing, sorting, reshaping, etc. However, SciPy executes computations, likewise numerical integration, optimization, and machine learning, operating NumPy's functionality.

Conclusion:

The world of data is massive, and its volume increases every day. According to a recent report, by 2021, there will be more than 20 billion connected devices. Every organization needs to have a strong data science strategy in such a scenario. The interdependence of different data sets, the need to analyze large volumes in real-time, and the increasing competition from the digital world show the importance of data science for organizations. It helps to make sense of all the data and present it in an organized manner to their stakeholders.

Data science is the practice and study of using data analysis and computational techniques to solve problems. If you want to make a career change and join the ranks of data analysis, you might be wondering what sets data science apart from other data-focused professions.

In addition to this, there is increasing interest in using programming languages other than JavaScript for creating rich internet applications. Python is a popular choice for building web applications. It has many advantages for building web applications and is an excellent language for beginners who are just getting started coding. It is an object-oriented programming language used to develop applications for desktop, server, mobile, and web. Python is widely used in software engineering, computational science, computer science education, and many others.

Data science and Python have numerous advantages, such as problem-solving skills. They help to find data that will help you solve data-driven problems. In addition to this, when you work with data, you will often face challenging tasks. You will need to use your problem-solving skills to figure out which data points you need to collect and then use your data-savvy skills to clean and organize that data. You often face tasks requiring you to analyze data stored on a computer or in the cloud. There is necessary to know how to use Python, a programming language that is easy to learn but can do almost anything you need.

Further, data analysis is an essential skill for workers in any field and an incredible way to make money online. You will often find data analysis jobs on websites like Upwork and Freelancer. By specializing in your skills, you will be able to find work quickly, and you might even start by doing side projects to build up a portfolio of work.

It is considered that data is the future, and it is what drives a lot of new technologies. Data plays a significant role in our lives, from self-driving cars to personalized medicine to ultra-accurate financial advice. This field is growing rapidly, and new possibilities are opening up every day. It is a very flexible field, and technological innovations often drive the work. You might work for online retailers, banking institutions, or even tech giants like Google.

Learning to work with data can also help you improve your skills in other areas. For example, you might become more aware of your strengths and weaknesses and even learn to approach problems from a different perspective. It can also be valuable for your mental health. By analyzing lots of data, you might gain a new appreciation for the randomness inherent in the world. It can help you relax and see the world differently, which can only be a good thing.

Working with data can help you stand out as a potential employee. For example, you might learn that you have a particular skill set that is valuable to an employer. Data can be a competitive advantage when you decide to pursue a career in data analysis. Working with data can help you stand out as a potential employee.

Thank you for taking the time to read the book! Your opinion matters, and your feedback can help other readers discover and enjoy the book as well. If you found value in this story, I kindly request that you share your thoughts and impressions by leaving a review on Amazon. Your review will not only support the author but also guide potential readers in making their decision. Simply click on the following link to share your review:

https://www.amazon.com/review/create-review/?ie=UTF8&channel=glance-detail&asin=B0BLBBNTV4

Thank you once again for your time, and I hope your review reflects the enjoyment you experienced while reading the book. Happy reviewing!

A FREE GIFT TO OUR READERS

7   surprising beginner mistakes you should avoid as a beginner programmer downloadable guideline. This will set you on the right path to learning how to program.

santosbooks.com

Made in United States
Troutdale, OR
12/06/2023

15405254R00124